TABLE OF CONTENTS

Unless otherwise indicated, all Scripture quotations are taken from the *King James Version* of the Bible.
Wisdom For Winning
ISBN 1-56394-218-6/B-01
Copyright © 1988 by *MIKE MURDOCK*
All publishing rights belong exclusively to Wisdom International
Publisher/Editor: Deborah Murdock Johnson
Published by The Wisdom Center · 4051 Denton Hwy. · Ft. Worth, Texas 76117
1-888-WISDOM-1 (1-888-947-3661) · **Website: thewisdomcenter.tv**

～ 1 ～

HOW TO ENJOY
THE WINNING LIFE

I Love To See People Succeed With Their Lives.

And so does God, the Creator. As the artist treasures his painting, and the master craftsman the quality of the violin he created, so our Maker cherishes the dreams, goals, excellence of life and the happiness you and I are to enjoy.

Success is being happy. And, happiness is basically feeling good about yourself, your life and your plans. Or, as one of my friends says, "Success is *joy!*"

Two forces are vital to happiness: your *relationships* and your *achievements.*

The Gospel has two forces: the *Person* of Jesus Christ, and the *Principles* He taught. You see, one is the *Son* of God, the other is the *system* of God. One is the *life* of God, the other is the *law* of God. One is the *King,* the other is the *kingdom.* One is an *experience with God,* the other is the *expertise of God.* One is *heart*-related, the other is *mind*-related.

Salvation is experienced *instantaneously;* God's Wisdom Principles are learned *progressively.*

Both forces are absolute essentials to total success and happiness.

You may be a church member and religious in

your experience, but you will live in continuous periods of frustration without the knowledge of the success laws established in the Scriptures. The expertise of God is a must in situations that arise in our daily living.

You may be a non-church member, an unbeliever. You may experience tremendous social, financial and family success and achievements through simple application of the Laws of Life as set forth in the Bible. But without the experience of Jesus Christ, the Son of God, you will always sense a vast void and loneliness, an awareness that "something is missing in my life." Job promotion, financial empire building and social acceptance will heighten and accentuate the emptiness rather than fill it. *God has not created a world He would not be needed in.*

Through searching diligently for principles for successful living, I was suddenly made aware of these *two forces*, the Person of Jesus and the Principles He set in motion. The *combined* power of these two influences I call the "Way of the Winner." The *system* I found in Scripture *worked*. It has multiplied my joy a thousand times over.

I wrote this book for you. I pray that each page will give you the added edge you need to make your life happier than ever before.

It is time to enjoy *Wisdom For Winning*. You deserve it, and God intended it for you. As you read this book, *mark* the pages and paragraphs that build you up. *Review* them each week. Make it *your* book...*Wisdom For Winning*.

Success is the *progressive achievement of God-*

intended goals. It is attainment of the will and plans *of the Father.* It is important that we have a *dream* or purpose in our lives. Joseph dreamed a dream. Jesus had purpose.

Our goals should be ordered of the Lord. David wanted to build the temple. But his desire was not a God-intended goal. Solomon was the builder God had chosen. Sometimes our personal desires are contradictory to God's plans.

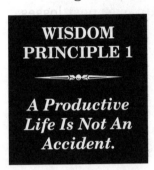

WISDOM PRINCIPLE 1

A Productive Life Is Not An Accident.

How do we know the difference? *Consultation* with the Father. Through the *Word* and private prayer time, we discover God's plans. Usually, it is revealed step-by-step.

If your desire for something *persists,* it probably is an indication that God wants you involved in that particular accomplishment. For example, God chose Solomon to build, but David *prepared* the materials.

Obviously, we must *know* what God wants us to do *before* we can do it. *Look* for signs. *Listen* to the Spirit. Evaluate. Cultivate *instant response* to the Voice of God. *Eliminate the time-wasters* in your life. Concentrate on your God-connection.

Reject all feedback and comments that breed doubt and defeat. Jesus did not give the same quality time to the Pharisees that He gave to the Samaritan woman. He discerned the *purpose of every conversation,* whether it came from a hungry heart or a critical attitude.

The Winner knows the power of words. Refuse

to release words of defeat, depression and discouragement. Your words are life. Express hope and confidence in God. Get so excited over planning your triumphs, you don't have time to complain over past losses.

The Winner expects opposition. Recognize that adversity has advantages. It reveals the depth of friendships. It will force you to dig for more accurate information. It will help you decide what you really believe.

WISDOM PRINCIPLE 2

Never Speak Words That Make Satan Think He's Winning.

The Winner expects special Wisdom to come. "If any of you lack wisdom, let him ask of God, that giveth to all men liberally, and upbraideth not; and it shall be given him" (James 1:5). Wisdom is the *ability to interpret a situation through God's eyes.* Wisdom is seeing what God sees. Understanding and Wisdom are the Golden Keys to mastering every circumstance in life. It comes through Word study. "The entrance of Thy words giveth light; it giveth understanding unto the simple" (Psalm 119:130).

WISDOM PRINCIPLE 3

Adversity Is The Breeding Ground For Miracles.

Winners are different from the "crowd." *Never* justify failure. Refuse to bog down in placing blame on others. Reach *up* for the key *out.*

Happiness begins between your ears. Your mind

is the drawing room for tomorrow's circumstances.
What Happens In Your Mind Will Happen In Time.

Mind-management is the first priority for the overcomer. "Whatsoever things are true, whatsoever things are honest, whatsoever things are just, whatsoever things are pure, whatsoever things are lovely, whatsoever things are of good report; if there be any virtue, and if there be any praise, think on these things" (Philippians 4:8).

Winners Are Simply Ex-Losers Who Got *Mad*.

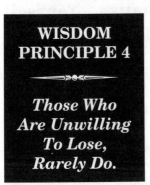

WISDOM PRINCIPLE 4

Those Who Are Unwilling To Lose, Rarely Do.

They got tired of failure. *The day you get angry at your failures is the day you start winning.* Winning doesn't start around you—it begins *inside* you.

Circle today's date on your calendar. Declare that the happiest and most productive days of your life are beginning today! Never, never, never quit. *You may be minutes from your miracle.*

When You Make Up Your Mind, It's Just A Matter Of Time

7 Secrets Of Personal Success

1.   **Define The Specific Goal You Want To Achieve.**

▶ Concentrate on one priority at a time. "This one thing I do,...I press toward the mark" (Philippians 3:13,14).

▶ Avoid distractions. "A double-minded man

is unstable" (James 1:8).

▶ Always secure assurance of the approval of God.

2.   Chart A Detailed Course With Established Deadlines.

▶ Write a detailed list of activities.

▶ Set checkpoints.

▶ Organize your time. "Redeeming the time, because the days are evil" (Ephesians 5:16).

3.   Constantly Visualize Yourself Attaining That Goal. What happens in your MIND will happen in time. "...whatsoever things are true,...honest,... just,...pure,...lovely,...of good report,...think on these things" (Philippians 4:8).

▶ "...calleth those things which be not as though they were" (Romans 4:17).

▶ Talk and think in "Success Pictures."

4.   Be Informed. Secure all pertinent information concerning your goal. "Wise men lay up knowledge:" (Proverbs 10:14). "My people are destroyed for lack of knowledge" (Hosea 4:6).

▶ Observe.

▶ Read. Maintain an "information file."

▶ Utilize the expertise of others. "He that walketh with wise men shall be wise:" (Proverbs 13:20).

5.   Create A Climate Of Confidence In Every Circumstance.

▶ Speak your *expectations* of *success*, not your *experiences* or *failures*. "Death and life are in the power of the tongue:" (Proverbs 18:21). Rehearse previous achievements in your mind. Remember that your sufficiency is of God. "In Whom we have *boldness* and access with *confidence* by the faith of Him" (see 2 Corinthians 3:5; Ephesians 3:12). Your position of superiority over circumstances was established when you became a child of God (see Romans 8:16,17,37).

6. **Help Others Become Successful.** Assist others in discovering their gifts, talents and dreams. You will reap what you sow. My personal motto came from the Holy Spirit over 20 years ago on the fifth day of a fast. It was 2:30 a.m. on a Friday morning as I prayed in my little garage/office in Houston, Texas— "What You Make Happen For Others, God Will Make Happen For You." When Job prayed for his friends, his captivity was turned (see Job 42:10). When the poor widow gave to the prophet, God gave to her (see 1 Kings 17). The Apostle Paul recognized this Law of Events. "Knowing that whatsoever good thing any man doeth, the same shall he receive of the Lord," (Ephesians 6:8).

> **WISDOM PRINCIPLE 5**
>
> ━━━➤●c━━
>
> *Life Changes Only When Your Daily Priorities Change.*

7. **Value The God-Connection.** Recognize God as a blessing factor. He is *never* a *disadvantage* to you, *always* an *asset*. He wants you to succeed and "...hath pleasure in the prosperity of His servant" (Psalm 35:27). Read the Scriptures on a daily schedule. Practice the power of prayer. Make

Jesus Christ Lord of your life. "Acquaint now thyself with Him, and be at peace: thereby good shall come unto thee" (Job 22:21). "...as long as he sought the Lord, God made him to prosper" (2 Chronicles 26:5).

~ 2 ~

HOW TO BE AN UP PERSON IN A DOWN WORLD

It intrigues the world. It is almost a phenomenon. What am I talking about?

An enthusiastic, happy person!

There is something magnetic and powerful about a victorious Christian. People are drawn to a consistent, excited believer!

Many write me and ask me in the crusades and seminars: "With today's problems—68,000 youth every day get V.D.; 1,200 new alcoholics every day! How can you keep your spirit *high* in a down world?"

> **WISDOM PRINCIPLE 6**
>
> *Happiness Occurs When You Move Toward Anything That Is Right For You.*

Believe me, *you can*. It is possible. Regardless of your family situation, your financial status, or past failures, you can step *up* into a Victory Zone and stay excited about life. Ephesians 2:6 says, God "...hath raised us up together, and made us sit together in heavenly places in Christ Jesus."

God intended for us to be

"*up*." He provided a plan to get us there. Spiritually. Mentally. Emotionally.

4 Things You Must Do As A Winner

1.   **Rebuild Your Concept Of God.** What is your idea and opinion of God? Is He a harsh dictator or a loving Father? Read Luke 15 and you will find a description of the Father *Jesus knew.* The

WISDOM PRINCIPLE 7

No One Has Been A Loser Longer Than Satan.

total obedience and respect Jesus had for His Father indicates His "God-picture" resulted in *trust.* Go beyond what you have heard or imagined about Him. *Read the gospels.* The nature, the compassion, the love of the *Father* is reflected through the *activities and attitudes of Jesus Christ.* Jesus took time to talk to an immoral woman...little children...a tax collector in a tree. *People mattered to Jesus.* Spend time developing the proper concept of God. Rebuild the mind-photo that strengthens your faith toward Him. By reading books, listening to cassette tapes and *sharing* your love with others, you will *correct* and *enlarge* your picture of God.

2.   **Recognize The Limitations Of Satan.** Certainly, there is a need to understand the damage of demonic influence. However, through the *Word* you will understand the *limitations* of their efforts. Satan is a liar. A deceiver. A manipulator. I might add that he is a loser. He is an *ex*-employee of Heaven who got "fired." He is headed for total destruction.

He is *under* the dominion of the believer, who is a joint-heir with Christ, Who has "...put all things under His feet," (Ephesians 1:22). Satan and the demon forces are *beneath us.* "We are *more than conquerors*" (Romans 8:37). *Remember,* you are the winner! When you feel you are at your lowest, you are still "on *top* of the devil!"

3.   Understand The Needs Of Others. Two classes of people who received attention from Christ were: First, people who *received* His ministry and His work. Good examples are Zacchaeus in Luke 19:2 and the Samaritan woman in John 4:9. Secondly, people who *ministered* to Him. Mary and Martha illustrate this in Luke 10:38.

Jesus' dealing with the Pharisees reveals they had a contempt, an irritation and absolutely no real respect for Him. They *neither ministered* to Him *nor received ministry* from Him.

Jesus saw people as *needs* that He could meet. If they received it, miracles happened. If rebellion surfaced, He detached Himself from them. He knew how to say no when necessary. *Cultivate discernment of people in your life.* If you are a *positive* influence on them, it will show. If you are not lifting them, chances are, they are a negative influence on you. "He that walketh with wise men shall be wise: but a companion of fools shall be destroyed" (Proverbs 13:20). Jesus could not spend time with

WISDOM PRINCIPLE 8

—➤●◄—

Those Who Do Not Respect Your Time Will Not Respect Your Wisdom Either.

everyone. He never gave "Zacchaeus Time" to be abused by the Pharisees. Develop the ability to listen to God in the part someone is to play in your life.

4.   Rebuild A Good Picture Of Yourself. Parents, schooling and friends condition us. We become failure-conscious. Sometimes we become more *problem*-oriented than *possibility*-oriented. We concentrate on our weaknesses and lose confidence and self-respect. *Begin to concentrate on your strong points.* Sometimes what you consider a weakness is actually a God-implanted gift.

> **WISDOM PRINCIPLE 9**
>
> *Stop Looking At What You See And Start Looking At What You Can Have.*

Let me illustrate. I've always loved to talk. My father was and is a very quiet man. I admired that. So I tried, with little success, to retrain my mouth to be quiet! I memorized Scriptures about talking too much. I suppressed my opinions in conversations. Oh, I admired and tried to emulate shy, timid, quiet friends. *Impossible.* I *had* to talk! Then, through my mother's and father's gentle and tender nurturing, they helped me see that God had given me a gift to express myself and make truths clear. I could study and work to make my words *edifying* and uplifting—a *strong point*. Since then, I've simply asked the Lord to give me words that will bless those around me!

Stop talking about your lacks. Be *thankful for gifts God has given to you!*

Listen to a preacher who wrote one-half of the

New Testament:

> ▶ "I can do all things through Christ"
> (Philippians 4:13).
> ▶ "Nay, in all these things we are more than
> conquerors" (Romans 8:37).

Paul had the right concept of *God*.

Paul had the right concept of *satan*.

Paul had the right concept of *people*.

Paul had the right concept of *himself.*

The Apostle Paul: God's idea of a winner. And Paul stayed *up*...in a down world!

Yesterday Is In
The *Tomb.*
Tomorrow Is In
The *Womb.*
Your Life
Is *Today.*

-MIKE MURDOCK

～ 3 ～

SEVEN OBSTACLES TO UNCOMMON SUCCESS

People Are My Life. And I have invested over 39 years of my life to increase their success and happiness through conferences, seminars, tapes and books.

Failure angers me. I rebel against unhappiness, sickness and hurt. Most of it could be *avoided* through recognizing and obeying the *Laws of God.* Much could be turned into a stepping stone to greater success if we knew how to *react* to situations.

7 Obstacles That Rob You Of Uncommon Success

OBSTACLE 1: AN UNTEACHABLE SPIRIT

An unteachable spirit is an *unwillingness to change.* Millions refuse to implement new and vital information as it becomes available.

Imagine a lawyer who refused to read new laws and *update his understanding.* Would you choose a surgeon who was unfamiliar with the latest medical technology?

The most successful businesses are those which adapt to new policies, produce new products and keep *informed.* They consult with experts. They analyze their own procedures. *Growing means change.* It's a part of prospering.

▶ "My people are destroyed for lack of knowledge" (Hosea 4:6).

▶ "A wise man will hear, and will increase learning;" (Proverbs 1:5).

▶ "If thou criest after knowledge...If thou seekest her as silver, and searchest for her as for hid treasures; Then shalt thou understand the fear of the Lord, and find the knowledge of God" (Proverbs 2:3-5).

A friend of mine has said, there are *two sources of knowledge:*

1.   **Wisdom**—learning from the mistakes of *others*, and...

2.   **Experience**—learning from *your own* mistakes.

Knowledge is exploding all around us. Uncommon men of God are sharing with us their expertise on faith, financial blessings and the power of God. They are teaching us many principles of success for marriage, purity and every part of our lives.

Books are crammed with information from years of research. *Cassette tapes* are made available for the price of a simple meal. *Magazines* are mailed free of charge.

God placed *Seeds of Greatness* within us at birth. *You* and I are responsible for *growing* those Seeds.

> **WISDOM PRINCIPLE 10**
>
> ———
>
> *Intolerance Of The Present Creates A Future.*

You are what you have decided to be.

If you are unhappy with yourself, *dare to reach* for *new* information, *new* teaching and *new* truths that will elevate you and build your relationship with God. If there is a sin in your life, repent and rededicate your life to Jesus Christ. Allow His precious blood to cleanse you. He will restore that fellowship you need with Him.

Invest in literature and teaching tapes. If your car is worth $30 for gas, surely your mind is worth growing! Don't bankrupt your mind! Don't starve your heart! Feed it what it desperately needs!

Dare to embrace change. Dare to listen to new ideas and concepts. God may want you on a new job, in a new city. Your best days are just ahead! *You can make it!*

WISDOM PRINCIPLE 11

Forgiveness Is Not A Suggestion, But A Requirement.

Recognize reasons for any failure. It is crucial that you locate the "bottleneck" in your life and activate the success and happiness that belongs to you.

OBSTACLE 2: UNPAID VOWS

Unpaid vows are the source of failure for many people. God *holds you responsible for your promises.*

▶ "When thou vowest a vow unto God, defer not to pay it; for He hath no pleasure in fools: pay that which thou hast vowed."

▶ "Better is it that thou shouldest not vow, than that thou shouldest vow and not pay" (Ecclesiastes 5:4,5).

Sometimes during a crisis you promise God that you will be faithful to attend church, or pay the tithe of your income, or to clear an offense with someone. Then afterwards, when you regain your health, you forget your vow. *This is deadly.*

It is important that you honor God and each other through honesty and the integrity of your words. You can give offerings, attend church and do many beautiful works, but if you allow a vow to go unpaid, it will destroy the *operation of faith* and the miracle God wants to perform.

Do you owe someone money? Make arrangements to pay, regardless how small those payments may have to be. "Bounced" checks are hardly a testimony to the provision of your Lord. What have you promised your *children?* Your *mate?* Your *company?* Are you fulfilling your vows? Have you really done your *best* to make things right with your creditors?

> **WISDOM PRINCIPLE 12**
>
> ⟞⟩●⟨⟝
>
> *Whoever Cannot Increase You, Will Eventually Decrease You.*

Dare to step out and take the responsibility for the vows you have made. God will honor you. You will sleep better. *Miracles* become daily events in the life of the obedient.

OBSTACLE 3: UNFORGIVEN OFFENSES

▶ "And when ye stand praying, forgive, if ye have aught against any: that your Father also which is in heaven may forgive you your trespasses. But if ye do not forgive, neither will your Father which is in heaven forgive your trespasses" (Mark 11:25,26).

Forgiveness is not a suggestion, it is a *requirement*.

It is *releasing to God the right to judge* and *penalize another for personal wrong.* Sometimes we feel we have a right to "pay back" a slight or injustice. This is *denying God the right to give mercy or penalty.* It is "playing God." God abhors the human urge to usurp His authority. Quit role playing! Let God judge and schedule punishment.

Visualize your offender as a hurt, damaged, wounded friend lashing out against you as a form of protection. He may be afraid of you and simply want to keep you from "getting the best of him."

Pray for those who have wronged you. Find a way to communicate a personal care and interest. Is it hard to do? Oh, very much so. But the personal *peace* it sets in motion is beyond description.

You have received mercy...sow it into others.

You have received love...sow it into others.

You have received kindness...sow it into others.

OBSTACLE 4: UNWISE ASSOCIATIONS

Solomon said it: "He that walketh with wise men shall be wise: but a companion of fools shall be destroyed" (Proverbs 13:20). Paul phrased it: "...evil communications corrupt good manners" (1 Corinthians 15:33).

Unwise friendships and associations have destroyed the potential and the abilities of multiplied thousands of could-be winners.

Disconnect from unqualified persons who abuse

and misuse your life. Jesus allowed only two kinds of people to absorb His time: first, those who *ministered* to Him and second, those who *received* His ministry to them. He knew that the Pharisees did not deserve His time because they abused it. *When someone does not value your time, neither will they value your Wisdom.*

Reevaluate your life and friendships. Do you allow your dreams to be eroded and your goals limited because of relationships with those who laugh at your pursuit of accomplishment? *Disconnect.*

I had an interesting revelation on this Principle of Power. A letter had been placed on my desk by my secretary as one worthy of "special attention." It was from a critical lady who had resented something I said in a meeting in which I was speaking. I spent one full hour trying to write a letter of explanation (really, an appeasement) to this lady. Suddenly, it dawned on me: I was spending more time on her than I had ever spent writing a letter to my precious mother who had supported and loved me for my entire life! I was actually giving *my time* — the most important commodity of my life — to someone who was completely unappreciative of such investment. I have stopped this practice and have focused instead on helping the thankful, not the critical.

4 Characteristics Of An Enemy

▶ *Those who are more critical than they are complimentary and encouraging.*

▶ *Those who belittle and laugh at your God-given dreams and goals.*

▶ *Those who embarrass and humiliate you.*
▶ *Those who drain your energy and waste your time through useless conversation.*

4 Qualities Of Wise Associations

▶ *Those who speak words that build your faith and confidence.*
▶ *Those who see the worthiness of your God-given dreams and goals.*
▶ *Those who become enthusiastic when you enter their presence.*
▶ *Those who remind you of your special gifts and abilities.*

You must choose the level of mentality you want to live on. If you give time to those unworthy of it, stop complaining. You are the one who gave them the time. They abused it because you allowed them the opportunity. Become more selective. Remember: the same time you waste on losers is that which could have been invested with winners.

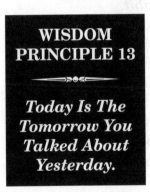

WISDOM PRINCIPLE 13

Today Is The Tomorrow You Talked About Yesterday.

OBSTACLE 5: UNBRIDLED TONGUE

▶ "Death and life are in the power of the tongue: and they that love it shall eat the fruit thereof" (Proverbs 18:21).
▶ "A fool's lips enter into contention... A fool's mouth is his destruction, and his lips are the snare of his soul. The words of a talebearer are as wounds, and they go

down into the innermost parts of the belly"
(Proverbs 18:6-8).

Words are *forces.*

Wrong or right, to build or destroy, words leave
a trail of destruction or accomplishment. Words can
build confidence or tear faith down.

Words are *tools* God gave you to build up your
own spirit and mind. Your *body* responds to *sounds.*
Your *spirit* responds to *words.* Words provide you
mind-pictures that your entire life reacts to.

You *hear* a story. You smile or cry. You *feel.*

What you *hear,* you *think* about.

What you *think* about, you *feel.*

What you *feel,* you *do.*

What you *do,* becomes a *habit.*

Your *habits* determine your life and eventual
destiny.

So, stop talking about shortages and setbacks.
Stop talking about defeat and disease. Stop talking
about failure and problems.

Concentrate on the opportunities at hand. Talk
about the blessings you now possess. Take time to
taste your triumphs today. *Now* is here.

Reach up. Take in. *Absorb* the beauty of *now.*
Talk about your *expectations,* not your experiences. *Talk*
about your *future,* not your failures.

Help others do the same. *Influence the conversations
around you.* Sometimes it is

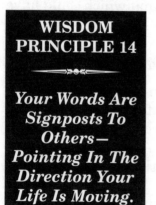

**WISDOM
PRINCIPLE 14**

*Your Words Are
Signposts To
Others—
Pointing In The
Direction Your
Life Is Moving.*

even good to "dominate your turf" with a little "aggressive happiness."

Happy people tend to be a little intimidating to the unhappy. The *Winner* seems *pushy* to a Loser. Dare to do it anyway. Their appreciation will be inevitable. When someone around you becomes ill, *pray* for them. When someone loses their job, *assist them* in stimulating their mind to find a creative alternative.

Control your mouth. "For by thy words thou shalt be justified, and by thy words thou shalt be condemned" (Matthew 12:37).

If you talk about all your losses, setbacks and failures, you are providing others with a photograph album and file of you *as a loser.* They will never see you as a Winner. Remember, every time you talk, you are *programming yourself* and *others.* Start conditioning your mind to accept your successes and triumphs.

A common mistake losers make is sharing their heartbreak stories *during* the period of loss. Winners never do that: They wait until that experience is *past* and share it as a *triumph.*

Instead of discussing people who are takers, *start concentrating on God. Your Giver.* You should memorize Matthew 7:7-11: "Ask, and it shall be given you; seek, and ye shall find; knock, and it shall be opened unto you: For every one that asketh receiveth; and he that seeketh findeth; and to him that knocketh it shall be opened. Or what man is there of you, whom if his son ask bread, will he give him a stone? Or if he ask a fish, will he give him a serpent? If ye then, being evil, know how to give good gifts unto your children, how much more shall your Father which is in heaven give good things to them that ask Him?"

Your *success future* is set in motion by your *words.* I like the way a friend of mine says it: *"There is a miracle in your mouth."* So, begin talking in the direction you want your life to move.

OBSTACLE 6: UNDEVELOPED GIFTS AND ABILITIES

Winners are people who have discovered their special talents, abilities and *special* God-given gifts. And, seeing their Seeds of Greatness, they have taken the time and energy to *grow* those Seeds into great benefits and advantages.

One secretary watches television all weekend, while another pursues an in-depth seminar study or develops her special shorthand skills. When it comes time for a raise or promotion, who has placed herself in the *position of advantage?* Certainly, the one secretary may complain that the other "gets all the breaks" or "the boss likes her" but in reality, one cultivated the gift God deposited in her Life-Account.

Our talents and abilities *differ.* "Having then gifts differing according to the grace that is given to us," (Romans 12:6). Though a man is compensated by other men according to their need for his special gift, God values every man's ability and gift equally. We must do the same.

If you enjoy working, do not play down your role as a secretary.

See the greatness of your gift. Take time to find it. Then, invest the time and effort necessary to improve it. The special talents God has given to you will generate everything you will need to be financially successful, but you must grow the Seeds within you.

Important Career Questions

What do you *enjoy* doing? What would you like to do *better*? What tasks do you *dread* doing? What brings you the *greatest* sense of fulfillment? Find out, and you will be well on your way to the sense of worth thousands have never taken the time to find.

Visit your library. Subscribe to periodicals. Consult the *experts* in the field of your interest. Set up appointments. *Pray* for divine direction. Respond to the opportunities in your local community for self-improvement and education. God will make the "shovel" available but you must start the "digging."

OBSTACLE 7: UNCOMMITTED HEART

"A double-minded man is unstable in all his ways" (James 1:8).

A committed heart is a decided heart. It is the result of a made-up mind. And it may explain the mystery of "charisma," or *presence,* that powerful people often generate when they walk into a room.

Commitment generates an aura of authority. It permeates an atmosphere. The effect is electrifying. Whether you are obsessed with evil as Adolf Hitler, or for righteousness as Billy Graham, *commitment* attracts people, favorable opportunities, and gives power and creativity to your life.

Get involved in something great and give your

life to it. Find something bigger than you are.
Connect with something you can really believe in.
If you are working for somebody you cannot respect,
find someone you can admire and attach your
Wisdom and energy to them.

Make a commitment to God. He made one to
you in the person of His Son, Jesus Christ. *Calvary
was commitment.* The blood and cross of Jesus was
commitment. Gethsemane was commitment.

Let's do something right now. Before you go
any further, pray this prayer with me aloud:

"Father, I *need* You. I believe You exist. *Forgive
me* for every sin I have ever committed. I *commit*
my life and heart to Your control. *Cleanse* my mind.
Free my heart to serve You. I make You Savior and
Lord of my life. I accept Your forgiveness, peace and
mercy with joy and a thankful heart. Use *me* to touch
another with Your special love. I *love You* with all
my mind, my heart and body. In the name of Your
Son Jesus, I pray. Amen."

∞ 4 ∞

TEN INGREDIENTS FOR SUCCESS

You Can Change The Course Of Your Life. A newcomer to town may fail to notice a traffic light and a collision results. Knowing the STOP and GO lights of life determines your *tears* or *triumphs.*

10 Power Keys For Stepping Up Into A Winner's World

1. **Discern The True Definition Of Success.** It is *not* necessarily popularity, possessions or prestige. Success is *the progressive achievement of a God-given goal.* It results in an *inner awareness that you are a worthy person.* Success results in happiness, really feeling good about yourself (read Mark 3:35; Joshua 1:7,8)!

2. **Set Definite Goals For Yourself.** God is a Goal-Setter. He scheduled the birth of a Savior and the Return of Christ hundreds of years *in advance.* It is not wrong to set goals. Jesus cautioned in Matthew 6 against *worrying* over them. James warned against *excluding God from them.* You do not merely set *your* goals, but set them under *divine guidance* (see Ephesians 5:17). *Deadlines* help you to redeem the time for the days are evil (see Ephesians 5:16). "A man's heart deviseth his way:

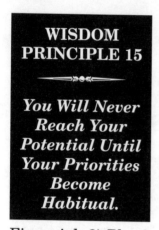

WISDOM PRINCIPLE 15

You Will Never Reach Your Potential Until Your Priorities Become Habitual.

but the Lord directeth his steps" (Proverbs 16:9).

3. Make Your Goals Balanced And Reasonable. Many fear the setting of goals because they think, "I might not make it." Don't make unreasonable expectations of yourself and others.

There are six basic areas of success: 1) Spiritual, 2) Financial, 3) Physical, 4) Mental, 5) Social and 6) Family. Overemphasis in one area often causes another area to deteriorate. You should be growing in all areas. Learn to break down big goals into smaller ones. "The wisdom of the prudent is to understand his way:" (Proverbs 14:8).

4. Meditate On Scripture. The mentality of God is absorbed through simply *reading the Word of God. Just read it.* Find an easy book like John. Read it, again and again. *Something will come to life inside you.* The Bible helps you to *think* as God thinks. It sharpens your response to the Holy Spirit. *It keeps you from falling.* Psalm 37:31 says, "The law of his God is in his heart; none of his steps shall slide." It gives you *discerning ability* for what is false, and what is true (see Psalm 119:130). I suggest that you read Psalm 1:1-3; Joshua 1:7,8; Psalm 119, for more encouragement in this area.

5. Discern The Spiritual Mentor That Most Increases Your Love For God. Do not attend a church just because of convenience, or because the preacher is a "nice guy." Listen to God.

Where does He want you? It may take you 30 minutes of driving instead of ten, but it can make the difference for the entire week! Invest a little time and research in finding the right church. Then, *be loyal.* Stand one hundred percent behind that church, its activities and your pastor (see Hebrews 10:25).

6. Pursue Quality People In Your Life. Spend time with winners. Be a learner. "He that walketh with wise men shall be wise;" (Proverbs 13:20). Pray and expect God to send uncommon people across your path.

WISDOM PRINCIPLE 16

Your Life Assignment Is Usually Whatever Creates The Highest Level Of Joy Within You.

7. Invest In Yourself. Spend time, effort and dollars in developing your *mind*, your *spirit* and your *inner* man. If a $20 meal makes your stomach feel good for four hours, think what it could do to your mentality and power-life to invest $20 in tapes or books that soak your mind and spirit in the anointing of God and give guidance in your life! Buy music tapes that fill your home and car with the presence of God! Hunters invest in guns. Nations buy tanks and weapons. *The successful person* is one who invests in equipping himself (see 2 Timothy 2:15).

8. Make Your Time Count. Time-wasters grieve God. People who sit around for hours joking and talking about nothing will guarantee your failure. Certainly, there is need for relaxation, recreation and fellowship. But America's obsession for *fun* is causing a deterioration of *purpose*. Idleness results in frustration, boredom and possibly even depression. Productive people rarely find time for depression (see Ephesians 5:16; Ecclesiastes 3:1-8).

9. Discover And Develop Your Own Talents. Find what you are good at, whether it's mechanical work, public speaking or artwork. *Take a good look at yourself.* Spend time finding out how to be the best at what you do. Most humans are born with abilities of some sort. You are accountable to God for developing your skills (see Matthew 25:14-30).

10. Cultivate A Teachable Spirit. Willingness to change is not necessarily a compromise of principles. Flexibility and openness to truth are evidence you are a winner. "A wise man will hear," (Proverbs 1:5). "As an earring of gold, and an ornament of fine gold, so is a wise reprover upon an obedient ear" (Proverbs 25:12).

Sometimes it takes courage to listen. Time and knowledge should *enlarge* you. Let it. *Listen.* Don't be a "know-it-all."

≈ 5 ≈

HOW TO FEEL GOOD ABOUT YOURSELF

"I don't know what is wrong," an attractive lady sobbed at a recent crusade. "My husband is so good to me. We live in a beautiful home...but I feel so frustrated. What do you think is wrong with me?"

I hate to see people unhappy. I hate to see people hurting inside.

What Is Happiness?

Happiness is *feeling good about yourself.* Do not confuse this with popularity, which simply means *others* feel good about you. But what you think about yourself, your character and your own accomplishments determines your real sense of worth and value.

Life is not a schedule of defeats, but a parade of miracles. It wasn't meant to be an endurance of trials, but an enjoyment of triumphs. *We decide.*

Jesus said, "These things have I spoken unto you, that My joy might remain in you, and that your joy might be full" (John 15:11).

Is happiness released by a Sunday morning walk to a church altar? Or repeating the "sinner's prayer" after a television pastor? Or by time spent with a marriage counselor? While many believers live in the joy and the power of the Jesus-life, others do not. Why are so many living in fear and defeat?

Too many are looking to someone else to bring their happiness to them. "But let every man prove his own work, and then shall he have rejoicing in himself alone, and not in another" (Galatians 6:4).

Happiness doesn't start *around* you, it begins *inside* you. *Stop waiting for flowers to arrive.* It is the growing of the Seed *inside* you this very moment. *Start growing the Seeds inside.*

Do You Feel Good About Yourself?

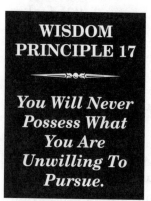

WISDOM PRINCIPLE 17

You Will Never Possess What You Are Unwilling To Pursue.

If not, *why not?* What bad news have you believed about yourself? Satan is the accuser of the brethren (see Revelation 12:10). Is he using a *past failure* in your life to destroy your faith?

One day I was praying. Suddenly, a mental photograph of a past failure leaped on the stage of my mind. It wasn't the first time satan had reminded me of that failure. I cried out, "Father, why does he keep using that same wrong over and over and over?" My Heavenly Father spoke so gently, "He's running out of material!"

Don't let past hurts and memories chain you to the *prison* of *defeat. Smash* the locks of your prison. Dare to resist the hurts and disappointments of yesterday. "Remember ye not the former things, neither consider the things of old. Behold, I will do a new thing; now it shall spring forth; shall ye not know it? I will even make a way in the wilderness, and rivers in the desert" (Isaiah 43:18,19).

Happiness is feeling *good* about yourself. Your sense of worth and value determine how good you really feel. Feeling good (or *happiness*) depends on *two* things:

1. **Your Relationships.**
2. **Your Achievements.**

You were built for connection. Your heart requires fellowship. Your mind demands negotiation. Your mouth longs for an ear that understands.

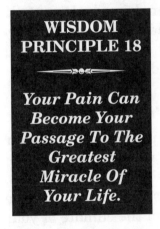

WISDOM PRINCIPLE 18

Your Pain Can Become Your Passage To The Greatest Miracle Of Your Life.

The Creator established your need for relationships. Relationships satisfy two huge needs of the human heart. *First,* the need to *receive* love. *Second,* the need to *release* love.

You have an inborn craving to make contact. That's why the wounded divorce victim still reaches out another time to risk love again, at the cost of emotional havoc. *Something in you always reaches for another*...even when your memory is screaming "anger!"

Relationships are a risk. They demand time, energy, attention and discipline. Like tender plants, they require patience before strength. Millions of people wither in loneliness, refusing to labor on the monument of love.

God-Relationship Is A Must

The *God-relationship* is a must. He created you.

He knows you so well. He has read every single sentence in your mind before you even think it.

God requires honesty. As well as holiness. In fact, *every miracle is preceded by the ache and agony of need.*

Like a child who rams the car into the telephone pole while trying to impress his father with his driving abilities, you sometimes have to splatter before you succeed. *You need Him.* I'd rather be His, *drawn* by His *blessing,* than *driven* by His *wrath. Jesus cried,* "...how often would I have gathered thy children together, as a hen doth gather her brood under her wings, and ye would not!" (Luke 13:34).

Family Relationships Are Vital

Your family relationships are vital to your happiness. The *Winner* is one who sees the *needs* of each member and strives to help fill that emptiness. *Time spent with your family is never wasted.* Wipe out criticism and sarcasm from the climate of your home. Be a confidence-builder. "Withhold not good from them to whom it is due, when it is in the power of thine hand to do it" (Proverbs 3:27).

Friendship Is Greater Than Gold

Friendships are greater than gold. They satisfy the inner part of us. Discern those orchestrated by the Holy Spirit and build them carefully, consistently and wisely.

Everyone needs to feel they have *achieved* something with their lives. When you stop producing, loneliness and laziness will choke all enthusiasm from your living. What would you like to be doing? What job could really turn on the excitement inside you? What are you doing about it?

Get started on a project in your life. Start building on your dreams. Resist those who would control and change your personal goals. You decide the goals God intended. Get going today! When you do, you will start feeling good about your life.

Happiness Is The Fragrance Of An Obedient Life.

Your Significance Is Not
In Your Similarity
To Another,
But In Your
Point Of Difference
From Another.
-MIKE MURDOCK

☞ 6 ☜

THE GRASSHOPPER COMPLEX

A few years ago, God gave me one of the most explosive concepts I have ever recognized.

The story is found in the book of Numbers. Moses was the leader of the Israelites. They had left Failure Zone (Egypt) and were headed for their Success Zone (Canaan). (Incidentally Canaan is not really a type of Heaven. It had giants, and Heaven contains none!)

Canaan is really a symbol of your dreams, your goals, your places of victories. It is "Success Territory." Every man should have goals of some sort. God intended for you to have them.

> **WISDOM PRINCIPLE 19**
>
> *You Will Never Reach The Palace Talking Like A Peasant.*

Abraham had a dream, Isaac.

Joseph had a dream, prime minister.

Solomon had a dream, the Temple.

The Israelites had a dream, Canaan.

Moses sent twelve spies, or scouts, to review the land before entering. The men saw the land, rich in honey, milk, grapes...and *giants*. When they came back, their reports were contradictory. Ten men had *evil* reports, two had *good* reports. Ignoring the giants was not what made their reports good or evil. All twelve recognized the existence of giants, even the two faith-spies Joshua and Caleb. *Faith-living is not ignoring the obvious.* Some people think if you recognize a problem situation, you are admitting doubt. That is incorrect.

Paul recognized once that satan hindered him (see 1 Thessalonians 2:18). Peter spoke of an adversary (see 1 Peter 5:8). Jesus, in Matthew 4, did not act as if satan did not exist. Ignoring a cancer or financial bondage or a marriage problem does not dissolve it. *You must admit something exists before you can confront it successfully.* The sinner is never converted until he admits his need. The Baptism of the Holy Spirit comes only to those who realize they are "empty."

WISDOM PRINCIPLE 20

Stop Looking At Where You Have Been And Start Looking At Where You Can Be.

All twelve spies had faith. But, there was a difference. Ten had faith in the giants. Two had faith in *God*.

Ten were giant-conscious.
Two were God-conscious.

Ten came back moaning, "Did you see the size of those *giants?*" Joshua and Caleb came back licking their lips, saying, "Did you see the size of those *grapes?*"

Ten were *"grasshoppers."*
Two were "giant-killers."
"Grape-tasters!"

Your *conversation* reveals whether you are a winner or a loser. Losers major on their problems.

Winners talk about the *possibilities*. Losers discuss their obstacles. Winners talk *opportunities*.

Losers talk disease. Winners talk about *health*. Losers talk about the devil's achievements. Winners talk about God's *victories*. Losers talk like victims. Winners talk like *victors*. Losers have a slaveship mentality. Winners have a *Sonship mentality*.

The Bible is a book of pictures. It gives you a picture of God, a picture of the devil and God's photograph of *you*. You will accept one of four possible evaluations of your life:

1. **What *You* Think About Yourself.**
2. **What *Others* Think About You.**
3. **What *Satan* Thinks About You.**
4. **What *God* Thinks About You.**

The ten spies said, "In our opinion, we are like grasshoppers. Even the giants think we are like grasshoppers."

I have heard many people talk as if they belonged to the First Church of the Grasshopper: "I'm nothing. I'm unworthy." A woman came up to me some time back saying, "Mike, I'm just nothing. I'm so unworthy."

I asked, "Did God create you?"

"Oh yes," she said.

I asked, "Do you think He puts trash together?"

She got the point.

God doesn't create cheap merchandise. You are His creation. You have worth. You have value. He implanted in you the Seeds of Success, faith

WISDOM PRINCIPLE 21

———◄►◄———

Your Words Are Deciding Your Future.

and power. Act like it. Live like it. Quit belittling yourself. Quit saying, "I'm stupid, I'm dumb."

Do you have the mind of Christ? Then you are super-brilliant! Say aloud, "I have the mind of Christ. I am amazed at the brilliant mind now in operation in my life." *You are no grasshopper! Quit talking like one! Quit living like one!*

Twenty-four years ago, in the midst of a traumatic situation, I began to weep before God. For three hours I sobbed as if my heart would break. Suddenly, the Holy Spirit said, *"Shut up!"* Have you ever had God talk like that to you? It is a bit strong! Even for this Irish lad.

I said, "But God, I'm weeping over what I have lost in my life."

He said, *"Get your mind off what you do not have. Get it on what you do have."*

Something exploded in my system. I had my mind on what I lacked instead of what I already possessed! There is a time to reach for that which you do not have...for that which seems impossible. *Then, there is a time to sit back and create a power climate of thanksgiving for what you possess now!* Quit magnifying your problems. Quit exaggerating the power of the devil. Start emphasizing the power of your *God!* Start testifying about the greatness of God, and what He is planning for you *today!* Start planning tomorrow's victories!

The *Grasshopper Complex will destroy your faith.* It will stop the faith flow. It will give satan a handle on your life.

Get the giant-killer instinct. You are greater than the enemy because you are a "God-House." He *lives inside you.* Quit looking at the failure photographs satan shows you of yesterday. God is keeping a photograph album of your victories, your future, your tomorrows! *God is not looking at where you stumbled yesterday, but at your possibilities tomorrow.*

The Grasshopper Complex is destroying the power of the local church today. It is paralyzing the faith flow. It is stopping the praise climate that God intended for us to create in the midst of our homes and our surroundings.

Too many talk like complainers instead of conquerors. *We are not grasshoppers.* The ten spies talked about the size of the *giants*—but Joshua and Caleb talked about the size of the *grapes!*

Focus on your opportunities, not the obstacles. Start praising God for what you *already* have—not just what you intend to have! If you are always reaching for that which is beyond your present possession, you will miss out on the joy of the "now" happiness—the "now" victory!

You can tell a *grasshopper* by his reaction to the greeting, "How are you?" He goes into the detailed "pain and hurt" routine. He talks about his health (or I should say his hurt, because few people go about telling how great their ears are hearing, their nose is smelling, their stomach is digesting, their eyes are seeing. They emphasize what is *wrong* instead of what is *right*).

Grasshoppers love to talk about the injustices of people toward them. They talk about how they have been mistreated, and how people do not understand them. Have you ever heard a grasshopper stand before a group and say, "I give all the credit to being a failure to myself?" Absolutely not! They have a list of people who caused them to be what they are. (I think I may have a few grasshopper tendencies. Do you?)

Grasshoppers justify their lack of victory. They always give excuses for not conquering the devil. In fact, they sometimes even put down others who are walking and living victoriously.

Grasshoppers constantly talk about their lack of finances. Giant-killers talk about their expectation of God's provision.

Grasshoppers refer to their children's ages as the "terrible twos." Giant-killers call that age the "tremendous twos."

I'm not saying it is easy. But to unleash the uncommon life, you must transfer from the *Grasshopper Complex to the giant-killer mentality.*

You must make up your mind to change. You can *change.* God has given you the *power of choice:* the power to direct your thinking; your actions! Make up your mind to *destroy* the "Grasshopper Complex."

Reinforce the giant-killer mentality by choosing friendships that build the faith life in you. You see, if you tolerate any other relationship it can be damaging to your spiritual growth. *Become choosey. Become selective. Become more particular* in the friendships you allow.

Discipline your *music,* your *television viewing,* your *reading material.* Use material that will build up your self-confidence as well as your dependency on the Lord and the life of the Spirit.

Dare to become assertive in spiritual things.

Dare to step out in faith. Dare to believe God for a new *mentality*. Dare to be positive about life, Dare to step *up...up...up...to a power life in God.*
Enter the Winner's World!

You Can Only
Conquer Something
You Hate.

-MIKE MURDOCK

~ 7 ~

BORN TO TASTE THE GRAPES

Man is born with a need to *win...to conquer.*

Slavery is *unnatural.* Our mind functions from the view of the predator, not the prey. We are built to *dominate* the works of God's hands. Thus, the lion and elephant are in the cage and man has become their keeper. "...Be fruitful, and multiply, and replenish the earth, and subdue it: and have dominion over the fish of the sea, and over the fowl of the air, and over every living thing that moveth upon the earth" (Genesis 1:28).

> ## WISDOM PRINCIPLE 22
>
> *A True Winner Will Never Advertise Nor Magnify His Personal Weaknesses.*

Man craves *greatness.* We possess an obsession to expand, to grow and to improve. We were born for the "high place." We instinctively gravitate toward *increase:* spiritually, mentally and financially.

The *"Seed of Need"* was planted by the Creator. God made Himself a *necessity* for human happiness. Like the missing puzzle piece, the life-picture does not make sense until He is included.

You were built for *connection.* The *ear* demands

sounds, the *eye* demands *sights,* the *mind* wants *imagination,* the *heart* seeks *companionship.*

The God-connection is the bridge from failure to success. Remember popularity is not success. Popularity is people liking you. Happiness is you liking you.

What Is Success?

Success is happiness. Happiness is feeling good about yourself. It is not necessarily fame, money or position. It is knowledge and awareness of your worth in the eyes of God.

You are here on purpose, designed and equipped for a particular function. You must discern and develop the God-given abilities He invested at your birth. It is only when those gifts are being used properly that you will feel and know the value God sees in you.

11 Benefits Promised From God

When possible sit and read the entire Book of Ephesians at one sitting. It is powerful. It tells us the respect and tenderness in which God views us as His children.

1.   He Has *Blessed* Us (1:3).
2.   He Has *Chosen* Us (1:4).
3.   He Has *Predestinated* Us (1:5).
4.   He Has *Accepted* Us (1:6).
5.   He Has *Redeemed* Us (1:7).
6.   He Has *Forgiven* Us (1:7).
7.   He Has *Abounded* Toward Us In Wisdom (1:8).
8.   He Has *Made Known* To Us The *Mystery* Of His Will (1:9).

9. He Has *Sealed* Us (1:13).
10. He Has *Enlightened* Our
    Understanding (1:18).
11. He Has *Raised* Us To Sit In Heavenly
    Places (2:6).

Think about it. Our Heavenly Father has *guaranteed* these 11 incredible blessings and benefits!

The great leader, Moses was a winner. He left us two fascinating verses in Deuteronomy 32:13,14 as he described God's dealing with His people in bringing them into greatness:

"He made him ride on the *high places* of the earth, that he might eat the *increase* of the fields; and He made him to suck honey out of the rock, and oil out of the flinty rock...and thou didst drink the pure blood of the grape." Picture this in your mind: "...drink *the pure blood of the grape.*"

You were born to taste the Grapes of Blessing. While some spend their lifetime discussing the size of their giants and problems, winners dare to reach up for the Grapes of Blessing God promised.

2 Important Principles In Tasting The Grapes Of Blessing

1. **The Grapes Are Not Merely For The Holy, They Are For The Hungry.** Many people feel like they are not good enough to receive the benefits of God. But remember, "...They that be whole need not a physician," (Matthew 9:12). The Pharisees never experienced the power and the glory of the Jesus relationship. It was the Samaritan woman, at the well, and Zacchæus, in the tree, who

were hungry for His touch, His blessing and His presence.

Maybe you have made a lot of mistakes in your life. Who hasn't? Some are perhaps more obvious! God knows your heart. He knows how desperately you want to start winning in your life. He wants you to taste the Grapes of *Favor,* the Grapes of *Prosperity,* the Grapes of *Health* even more than you could ever want them!

Stop looking at your weaknesses.

Start concentrating on the *strengths* He has given you. Stop looking backward. (You can't go fast looking through the rear view mirror!)

"Oh, but Mike, you just don't know the mess I am in!" one lady cried.

"You don't drown by *falling* in the water, you drown by *staying* there," I replied.

Get up from your situation. Start setting your success in motion.

2. The Grapes Are Not Placed Within Your Mouth, They Are Placed Within Your Reach. Nobody wakes up successful and happy. Many people think, "Well, if God wanted me healthy, I'd be healthy. If God wanted me financially prosperous, I'd be that way. God is in control."

What does God control?

He controls the laws of this universe.

He does *not* control your *decisions!*

And your decisions are creating your circumstances!

Stop assigning to the sovereignty of God the responsibility for all of your situations. Use the mind and abilities God has given you to create *new* and *better* circumstances. Go after the job He created you for. Take care of the body He has given to you.

The Grapes exist, but you must *reach* for them.

7 Gates To The Grapes Of Blessing

You were born to taste the Grapes, born to enjoy royalty, and the blessings and benefits of God. You have the *instinct for improvement*. You have a motivation for increase. *Something inside you gravitates toward growth*. You were created for expansion. God created you that way, and you will never be happy any other way.

Now, I could discuss forever these Grapes and how luscious and tasty they are. Grapes of *Wealth, Health, Peace, Power, Success*— but unless you know how to obtain the Grapes, it will not help you.

1. The Gate Of Obedience.

Deuteronomy 28:1 says, "...if thou shalt hearken diligently unto the voice of the Lord thy God," This simply means *doing what God has told you to do*. It means living up to the knowledge you have received. If you are a *gallon,* live up to gallon knowledge. If you are a *pint,* live up to pint knowledge. You can move into states of perfection and maturity as God reveals Himself to you. Abraham was called a *friend* of God *because he obeyed God.*

God said, "Abraham, I want you to move from your comfortable situation and go to a new country." Abraham *obeyed* God. If God has been talking to you about something, *do it*. Don't negotiate.

That raises a question: How can we know The Voice of God? It is impossible to describe The Voice of God. Oh, I could give you some guidelines, but when it comes to *knowing* when God is speaking, you have to become addicted to Him. I don't have to ask, "I wonder if this man is my brother." I know his voice. If you have spent time in the presence of God, you will know His Voice.

If God is drawing you, speaking to you and dealing with you, *obey Him.* It may even appear to be a step backward. It may be something you do not really want to do. But if you will say, "Father, I will do what You ask me" and will step through the Gate of Obedience, all of Heaven will open for you. God is standing by the windows of Heaven ready to pull them open and unload an avalanche of Blessings if you will just obey Him (see Malachi 3:10). He said, "If ye abide in Me, and My words abide in you, ye shall ask what ye will, and it shall be done unto you" (John 15:7). Oh, unleash the powerful benefits of obedience!

2.   The Gate Of Knowledge.

God says, "My people are destroyed for lack of knowledge" (Hosea 4:6). What you do not know can

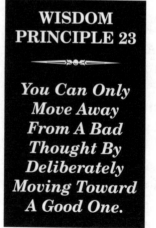

WISDOM PRINCIPLE 23

You Can Only Move Away From A Bad Thought By Deliberately Moving Toward A Good One.

destroy you. God wants you knowledgeable. *Information is God's business.* All of Heaven is involved in distributing information. Angels bring information. The Bible is an information manual. It is literally the *"Winner's Digest,"* informing us about God—His power, nature and thoughts about us—and about satan, angels and demon spirits.

You have a right to the blessings of God. You are a child of the Most High God, an heir of God, a joint-heir with Jesus; He is your *elder brother.* You have a right to enter in the Holy of Holies. You have on your behalf a *High Priest,* an *Intercessor* beside the right hand of the throne of God. But you cannot take hold of the grace and blessings of God unless you have *knowledge* of what He has provided for you. I am saying that *you have to know what belongs to you.* You must open and walk through the *Gate of Knowledge.* "But without faith it is impossible to please Him: for he that cometh to God must believe that He is, and that He is a rewarder of them that diligently seek Him" (Hebrews 11:6).

A woman came forward for prayer one night, and I asked her, "Do you want God to heal you?"

"Well," she responded, "I think He is trying to show me something." Imagine such ignorance!! Have you ever heard of *"Disease University?"*

Many people have accepted disease and sickness as teachers. The Bible says that the *Holy Spirit will lead you into all truth.* Not, "Yea, I will send disease and it will teach you and lead you into all truth."

Know what the Word of God says, and believe it. Pray, "God, Your Word says that You were wounded for my transgressions, bruised for my iniquities and by Your stripes I am healed" (Isaiah 53:5). Embrace the Word and stand upon it. You can spend your energy *explaining your sickness,* or you can spend your energy *reaching for a miracle.*

Do you have a thorough knowledge of the

Grapes God has provided? Find out what the Scriptures teach; know about the Grapes you are reaching for. A lot of people have not because they do not even know the Grapes exist. You were born to taste the Grapes and you need to have the knowledge that God made them available and accessible to you.

3.   The Gate Of Visualization.

Visualize the Grapes. If you cannot see the Grapes in your *mind,* you will not see them in your future. Your mind is a force that affects everything else in your life. *The renewing of your mind is the secret of transformation* (see Romans 12:1,2). Your mind is a powerful force.

The woman with the issue of blood said to herself, "If I may touch but His clothes, I shall be whole" (Mark 5:28). She visualized. *It happened in her mind before it happened in her body.* Visualize the Grapes. See yourself tasting the Grapes. See yourself with victory. Some of you have never seen yourself victorious like God means for you to see yourself. Visualize where God wants you to be. Then, act as if you are *already* there.

WISDOM PRINCIPLE 24

You Cannot Reap Grapes Until You Have Sowed Grapes Into Others.

Jesus visualized Himself in victory: "...for the joy that was set before Him [He] endured the cross," (Hebrews 12:2). He endured the present suffering for the joy that was set before Him; His mind was picturing victory. When Jesus walked to Calvary, He was not looking at the cross;

WISDOM PRINCIPLE 25

Praise Lifts You To Where God Is.

He was looking at the *resurrection*.

If you have always longed to be victorious in an area, *get your mind on the Grapes* until you can visualize them and see them in your grasp. Is there a habit in your life you want to conquer? *Do not* concentrate on the habit; *concentrate on victory*. This is called the *Law of Displacement*. It means you *displace* evil by the *entrance* of good. We do not go into a building and suggest to darkness, "Would you mind leaving, because if you leave we can have light?" We bring in light, and the *entrance of light forces the exit of darkness*.

Some people spend their lives saying, "Oh, I wish I could quit thinking bad thoughts." You'll never stop thinking bad thoughts, you'll never stop thinking doubt, until you *start* thinking faith and you start seeing yourself victorious. That picture drives out evil. Visualize it right now. Whatever it is, see yourself with it.

4. The Gate Of Forgiveness.

The fourth Gate to the Grapes is Forgiveness, which simply means *the transferal of the right to judge and penalize*. It means that you give up your position on God's vengeance team. *Forgiveness does not flow to you until it can flow through you.* You can ask for forgiveness, beg God for forgiveness, offer Him "double tithe," but nothing will happen inside you until you permit God alone to penalize others for doing you wrong.

"Well, Mike, I want to teach him a lesson."

That's understandable, but it is wrong. God is the One in charge of payment; He is the Judge. Exercise the ability to *withhold* judgment and let God perform His program of restoration and forgiveness.

Forgiveness is the removal of information and the pain of it. There is no entry into Heaven until you walk through the Gate of Forgiveness. There are no Grapes of Blessing, no Grapes of Reward, until you "remember...not the former things" (Isaiah 43:18).

Forgive not only other people, but forgive yourself. That is just as important. There are people who have never forgiven themselves. *Never advertise your mistakes.* Lay the memory of them at the cross and *leave them there.* Jesus is your sacrifice!

5. The Gate Of Persistence.

What is the Gate of Persistence? Simply make up your mind, regardless of how far away the Grapes appear, to push on for the blessing. Sometimes it will seem like they are a thousand miles away. Friends may try to discourage and disillusion you. They may not understand your dream, your goal. It will not fall into your lap automatically. It will not be easy. But every man or woman who has ever achieved anything had to *persist.* They made up their minds to go after what they believed in.

I met a young man the other day—sharp, nice. He could be a great preacher. Will he ever be? I doubt it. Why? No persistence: "I tried and it didn't work. I think I will quit. I don't know if I am called."

The power belongs to the persistent. For ten days

the disciples waited in the Upper Room. Can you imagine the first day? Someone says, "Well, He said for us to just wait; here we are." Second day, third, fourth, fifth, sixth. Another says, "You know, if God *really* wanted us to have power, He wouldn't make us just sit here and wait for it." Seventh day. Eighth. Ninth. Tenth—suddenly, a sound from Heaven as a rushing mighty wind fills the room (see Acts 2:2). Cloven tongues of fire sat upon their heads, and they began to speak in tongues as the Spirit of God gave them utterance. Why? *Persistence.*

Say it: *"Persistence."* Say it until your whole body feels it. There will be times you will not feel like you can make it. At times you will feel like asking, "Why am I doing this anyway?" Or, you will feel like "it's no use, nothing is going to work out." Stay there! The diseased woman did not feel like pushing her way through the crowd, *but she had a goal.* I am certain Peter did not always feel like an overcomer, but God gave him such a victory that when he, the man who had denied the Lord, began to preach he said, "You folk need to repent; you denied the Holy One of Israel" (see Acts 3:14). *He persisted until the power of God came into his life,* and he walked in that power.

6. The Gate Of Sowing.

You cannot have Grapes until you *sow* Grapes. The blessing *follows* the Blesser. *Whatever good thing you do for another, God is going to do for you* (see Ephesians 6:8). If you want to taste Grapes, you have to distribute Grapes. You have to bless *other* people if you want God to bless *you.*

If you want something good to happen in your

life, you must make something good happen for your sister or brother. You must first perform for *others* what God wants to perform for you.

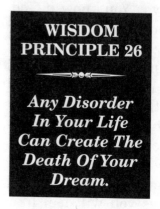

WISDOM PRINCIPLE 26

Any Disorder In Your Life Can Create The Death Of Your Dream.

Jesus did not say that if you treat your brother or sister right he or she will love you. He said that if you do right to others, *God* will do right by you. Everything reproduces after its own kind. If you want healing, start praying for *others* to experience healing. If you want blessings, start concentrating on *others'* receiving their blessing. Jesus concentrated on other people's needs. He went around doing good, healing all that were sick and oppressed of the devil (see Acts 10:38). What You Make Happen For Others, God Will Make Happen For You.

7. The Gate Of Praise.

Judah, which means *praise,* was the first tribe into battle. Praise is the sound that makes hell sick; it unnerves demons. Satan used to be the song leader in Heaven, but God kicked him out. Anytime you start praising God, all of Heaven notices it. Let the redeemed of the Lord say so! Make a joyful noise! Clap your hands.

Praise is an act of the will. It is not something you have to *feel* in order for it to be real. It is *not* meditation; it is something that is *heard.* Praise is articulated sound and opinion. It is your *recognition* of Jesus as Lord of everything, that Jehovah is still on the throne.

When you begin praising God, something miraculous happens. I don't care how you feel; if you start saying, "God, I love you," something *loosens.* Talk about smashing the locks of your prison; *praise* does that! Now, praise has nothing to do with feelings. You don't have to say, "God, I feel great," or, "I feel lousy." Praise has to do with *Him* and *it takes your mind off yourself.*

Praise lifts you to where God is.

God is very comfortable with praise. In fact, that is where He chooses to *dwell* (see Psalm 22:3). God likes praise, and He *responds* to it. Not only does God respond to praise, demons repulse at it.

Praise is something you deliberately *choose to do*, to acknowledge the power of God.

Now, the purpose of praise is not just to make you feel good, but it is also to stir others. God values recognition. He does things in a big way. You never see God "sneaking" around saying, "You be quiet now and have a good time." He is a *celebration* God, an *expressive* God.

You were born to taste the Grapes of God's blessing. The silver and gold are His. He gives us

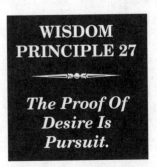

WISDOM PRINCIPLE 27

The Proof Of Desire Is Pursuit.

the power to get wealth. Everything that God has, everything that He is, He is willing to pour *into* us and *through* us. The Grapes are not for the holy, they are for the *hungry.* They are not placed within your mouth; they are placed within your reach. So, enter the Gates and reach for the Grapes. They are *accessible... today.*

The Proof Of Desire
Is Pursuit.

-Mike Murdock

≈ 8 ≈

YOUR GOALS AND HOW TO ACHIEVE THEM

One of the major causes of failure is the unwillingness to take the time to determine your true goals.

It is also a very misunderstood practice. Some think that the Bible teaches against planning ahead, using Matthew 6:25 and James 4:13-15 as their basis. However, the concern Matthew dealt with was worry, not the setting of goals. James was referring to the setting of goals without God's involvement.

4 Reasons Some Never Set Goals

1. **Some Have Not Tasted The Joy That Goal Setting Produces.**

2. **Some Do Not Know How To Write These Goals Down With Clarity.**

3. **Some Are Afraid Of Possible Failure.** (If we do not set a goal, there is no guilt or negative feelings of not reaching it!)

4. **Some Fail To Set Goals Because Memories Of Previous Failures Intimidate Them.** Perhaps their goals were too unreasonable.

At any rate, I want to help you understand the wonderful victories accomplished through *written* goals.

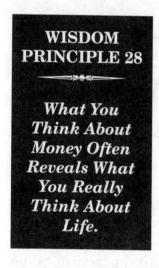

WISDOM PRINCIPLE 28

What You Think About Money Often Reveals What You Really Think About Life.

In the Old Testament, Abraham's father, Terah, set a goal of making Canaan his residence. Later, Abraham accomplished this goal with his nephew, Lot (see Genesis 11, 12). In the New Testament the Apostle Paul planned to "winter" with the Corinthians (see 1 Corinthians 16:6), and to spend another winter in Nicopolis (see Titus 3:12). In Proverbs 16:9 we are told: "A man's heart deviseth his way: but the Lord directeth his steps." Proverbs 14:8 says: "The wisdom of the prudent is to understand his way."

Planning cures disorder.

One outstanding lesson on planning ahead is given in Luke 14:28-30: "For which of you, intending to build a tower, sitteth not down first, and counteth the cost, whether he have sufficient to finish it? Lest haply, after he hath laid the foundation, and is not able to finish it, all that behold it begin to mock him, Saying, this man began to build, and was not able to finish".

The setting up of specific goals is one good way of fulfilling the *purpose* God has for your life. For instance, you might *purpose* to be a better Christian this year. That is general. To fulfill that purpose your daily goal would be to read a specific amount of chapters in the Bible *each day,* set up a *morning prayer time* and so on.

Goal-setting takes time, discipline, courage and

patience. There are temptations along this line. Sometimes we let others dictate our personal goals instead of deciding for ourselves. Some people become comfortable in a particular job and stay with it for 20 years even though *they may be missing a Divine position God is wanting to transfer them to.* Financial security to them is their job, not their Heavenly Father.

5 Steps In Achieving Your Goals

1.   **You Must Decide For Yourself What You Really Want Out Of Life.** Nobody else can decide for you. If you do not care what happens to your life, no one else will.

2.   **Get Alone With God And His Word.** This enables you to understand His plan and what He desires. This is getting "in agreement" with His will and purpose. This helps you to *avoid* setting the *wrong* goals.

3.   **Write Down On A Sheet Of Paper Every Single Dream, Goal And Desire That Is Presently Important To You.** Write down anything that you have ever wanted to *do, become* or *possess.* It may be spiritual, physical, mental, financial or have to do with family. It is important that you *write* it down. (Do not leave it in your mind!) "The shortest pencil is better than a long memory." As my brother John has said. "Faintest line is better than strongest mind."

4.   **Choose The Top Three Goals Out Of The Long List.** Now write down at least *five* actions you can do *now* toward accomplishing that *big* priority goal. Remember, a *big success* is simply

several little successes linked together.

5.   Be Alert To The People God Will Send Into Your Life To Help You Fulfill His Purpose, And Be Responsive To Obey God When He Directs Your Talents To Help Fulfill The Dreams Of Others. This simply restates my basic motto that God gave me during a five-day fast in 1977: "What You Make Happen For Others, God Will Make Happen For You."

≈ 9 ≈

TEN LIES MANY PEOPLE BELIEVE ABOUT MONEY

One of the needs people write me about most is their financial problems. I know what it means to prosper and I also know what it means to be completely wiped out financially.

One of the tools satan uses to destroy incentive, goals, and joy of accomplishment is financial difficulty. I wrote this book because I care about you and the losses you may experience in life. Read this chapter with an open mind toward God and how you can become a winner in the financial area of your life.

> **WISDOM PRINCIPLE 29**
>
> *Whatever You Think About Most Is Really Your God.*

Chilling screams of terror tore into the cold night air. The explosion of metal. Helpless cries of torment and desperation. Families wiped out. Lifetime dreams shattered like glass upon concrete. Emotional scars forever engraved on the soul. Havoc. Destruction. Chaos. All in a matter of minutes.

Because somebody lied.

In the rush, the plane mechanics had failed to notice the tiny malfunction. Signaled that all was well, the pilot proceeded down the runway. *He accepted the opinion and judgment of others.*

It cost him his life.

Your happiness depends on something you are believing. Success or failure depends on your believing a lie or the truth. In marriage, in health, in spiritual matters and even in finances, what you believe makes *all* the difference. From Santa Claus to tooth fairies, all of us can remember moments we believed a lie. Sometimes harmless, sometimes devastating.

One of the greatest needs of life is *money.*

▶ Sit with the minister counseling the young married couple—*money.*

▶ Look at the youth in prison for stealing—*money.*

▶ Listen to the missionary from Africa sharing the needs of his ministry—*money.*

▶ Talk to the weary overworked husband—*money.*

▶ Read the Holy Bible. The teachings of Jesus Christ include this power topic—*money.*

Thousands live unfulfilled and frustrated lives because they do not understand the truth about money.

10 Lies Many People Believe About Money

LIE 1: *Money is unimportant.*

Recently, I sat in a coffee shop in the Dallas-Fort Worth airport. I listened as the waitress spoke of her long hours, small apartment and two children.

"Wouldn't you like to be making more money?" I asked.

"No, I would not!" She replied indignantly. "That's what is wrong with our world now: greed. I have enough for my bills and support for my two kids, and that's all I want. People place too much emphasis on money. *Money is unimportant.*"

I could hardly believe my ears.

"Have you ever heard of Calcutta, India?"

"Yes," she replied.

"Have you ever seen pictures of the starving children there?"

"Yes."

"Have you ever sent them any money or food?"

"No."

"Why not?" I asked.

"I haven't had enough..." Her voice trailed off.

I could see in her eyes the truth had dawned. Money *does* count. Life hinges on it. *Money is the power part of our world.* With it we bargain, trade and exchange our way through life! Shelter, food, medical care, education and even self-preservation involve money. Money is a basic method of communication between human beings. In war or peace, love or hate, *money talks.*

LIE 2: *Money is evil.*

Many people misquote the Bible verse when the Apostle Paul wrote Timothy: "For the love of money is the root of all evil:" (1 Timothy 6:10). It does not say that money is evil, but that the love of or obsession for money is the root or beginning of evil. Why? Because the love of money is *idolatry.* It is the worship of the creation instead of the Creator.

God is the owner of wealth. Haggai 2:8 says: "The silver is Mine, and the gold is Mine, saith the Lord of hosts".

God is the Giver of wealth. Deuteronomy 8:18: "But thou shalt remember the Lord thy God: for it is He that giveth thee power to get wealth".

When God gives you a gift, it must have value, importance and purpose for your life: "Every good gift and every perfect gift is from above, and cometh down from the Father" (see James 1:17).

God would never give evil gifts to His children.

It is the *misuse* and *abuse* of money that can be destructive. Not money itself. For example, *fire* destroys homes, beautiful forests, kills human beings. Yet properly controlled, it is a tremendous tool for cooking food, warming houses and running automobile engines. *Flood waters* have drowned many human lives. Yet, water is necessary for human life. Cleanliness and even nature depend on it. So, it is with *money.* It can be used *for good!* As one humorist has said, "Money is not cold, hard cash, but warm, soft blessings!"

LIE 3: *Money never hurt anyone.*

This truth is undeniable: *Money will affect you.* Why? What is behind the mysterious magnetism of gold? Men have killed for money. Men have deserted children and wife in search of gold. You see, the basic craving of man is a *sense of worth,* a sense of importance. Money represents *power,* influence, achievements and security. That is why money can be deceptive. Jesus referred to this as the *"deceitfulness of riches"* which arrested spiritual development (see Matthew 13:22). It is a false sense

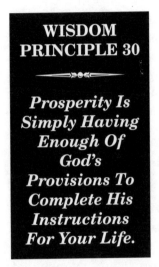

WISDOM PRINCIPLE 30

Prosperity Is Simply Having Enough Of God's Provisions To Complete His Instructions For Your Life.

of security. A wise and wealthy ruler advised, "For riches are not for ever" and, "...riches certainly make themselves wings; They fly away as an eagle toward heaven" (Proverbs 27:24; Proverbs 23:5).

Money often produces pride. This is spiritually devastating (see Mark 10:25). Whatever consumes your time, whatever you think about most is really your "god" (see Matthew 6:24). God refuses to compete, and guarantees that "He that trusteth in his riches shall fall:" (Proverbs 11:28). Yes, money can hurt you.

LIE 4: *Money would cure your problems and guarantee personal happiness.*

Unfortunately, the opposite is true in many cases (see Ecclesiastes 5:12). The rich sometimes feel that their friendships are fragile and plastic, based on their possessions and not themselves. Bitter, frustrated and lonely, some have even committed suicide.

Think for a moment. Are you still content with your last salary increase? Probably not. Ecclesiastes 5:10 says: "He that loveth silver shall not be satisfied with silver;...Neither is his eye satisfied with riches" (Ecclesiastes 4:8). It is having a *purpose* in life, not possessions, that is truly satisfying. And that purpose can only be realized in the person, Jesus Christ. "He that hath the Son hath life; and he that hath not the Son of God hath not life" (1 John 5:12).

Unbelievers often ignore the *problems of prosperity*.

Believers often ignore the *purpose for prosperity*.

Whether it is the deterioration of a marriage, or the moral fiber of an entire nation, man's basic problem is *spiritual*.

LIE 5: *Some are gifted for wealth and some are destined for poverty.*

This ridiculous lie has destroyed initiative, drive and motivation in many would-be winners throughout the world. Many capable people have believed, "Whatever *is*, was *meant* to be." *Nonsense!*

The truth is, through development of your God-given *talents* and the principles of *giving,* you determine the financial Harvest of your life.

> ▶ "He that tilleth his land shall be satisfied with bread:...The hand of the diligent shall bear rule: but the slothful shall be under tribute" (Proverbs 12:11,24).

> ▶ "In all labour there is profit: but the talk of the lips tendeth only to penury" (Proverbs 14:23).

> ▶ Jesus said, "Give, and it shall be given unto you" (Luke 6:38).

> ▶ Solomon said, "There is that scattereth, and yet increaseth; and there is that withholdeth more than is meet, but it tendeth to poverty. The liberal soul shall be made fat: and he that watereth shall be watered also himself" (Proverbs 11:24,25).

God explained that financial curse or financial blessing depended on the *attitude of obedience:*

"*Blessed* shalt thou be" (Deuteronomy 28:1-14) or "...cursed shalt thou be" (Deuteronomy 28:15-68). Malachi 3:8-11 reveals the reason many are not prosperous. "Will a man rob God? Yet ye have robbed Me. But ye say, Wherein have we robbed Thee? In tithes and offerings. Ye are cursed with a curse: for ye have robbed Me, even this whole nation."

▶ "Bring ye all the tithes into the storehouse, that there may be meat in Mine house, and prove Me now herewith, saith the Lord of Hosts, if I will not open you the windows of heaven, and pour you out a blessing, that there shall not be room enough to receive it."

▶ "And I will rebuke the devourer for your sakes, and he shall not destroy the fruits of your ground; neither shall your vine cast her fruit before the time in the field, saith the Lord of hosts."

LIE 6: *God does not want you to be financially prosperous.*

This is absurd! The *necessities* of our lives, and the *needs* of others demand financial blessings. Jesus assured us, "...your heavenly Father knoweth that ye have need of all these things" (Matthew 6:32). The apostle Paul denounced the man who would not provide for his family: "But if any provide not for his own, and specially for those of his own house, he hath denied the faith, and is worse than an infidel" (1 Timothy 5:8).

God Is Your Source

"If ye then, being evil, know how to give good

gifts unto your children, how much more shall your Father which is in heaven give good things to them that ask Him?" (Matthew 7:11).

God Gives Wealth

"But thou shalt remember the Lord thy God: for it is He that giveth thee power to get wealth" (Deuteronomy 8:18). He promised Solomon: "...I will give thee riches, and wealth" (2 Chronicles 1:12). God "...hath pleasure in the prosperity of His servant" (Psalm 35:27).

Money is a tool. While money may become a *snare* for the unbeliever, it is the Christian's *tool for evangelization.* You see, there are two types of achievers in the Christian world...

1. **Those Who GO.** "And He said unto them, Go ye into all the world, and preach the gospel to every creature" (Mark 16:15).

2. **Those Who SEND.** "How then shall they call on Him in Whom they have not believed? and how shall they believe in Him of Whom they have not heard: and how shall they hear without a preacher? And how shall they preach, except they be sent? as it is written, How beautiful are the feet of them that preach the gospel of peace, and bring glad tidings of good things!" (Romans 10:14,15).

Money in the hands of Christians is a threat to satan. As we spread the gospel, the timing of the return of Christ is even affected.

Satan's period of power can be shortened when believers use prosperity as a tool for God's work! "And this gospel of the kingdom shall be preached in all the world for a witness unto all nations; and then shall the end come" (Matthew 24:14). Through our giving, missionaries are sent, Christian television and radio stations established, churches built and Bibles printed. Prosperity is much more than Rolls Royces and palaces. *Prosperity is having enough of God's supply to complete His instructions for your life—enough of His provisions to accomplish His commands and expectations.*

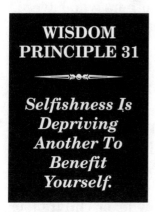

WISDOM PRINCIPLE 31

Selfishness Is Depriving Another To Benefit Yourself.

LIE 7: *There is nothing you can do about your financial situation.*

While losers wait for some "magic moment of luck," the Winner works God's Principles of Prosperity. Your financial circumstances depend on three factors:

- ▶ *Spending*: following God's timing for *purchases,*
- ▶ *Saving*: the discipline of planning ahead (see Proverbs 6:6), and
- ▶ *Sharing*: releasing offerings into ministries in the work of God for the spreading of the gospel (see 2 Corinthians 9:6).

Your Credit Cage

Learn to break the bars of the credit cage. "The borrower is servant to the lender" (Proverbs 22:7). Impulse buying and pride-motivated purchasing can paralyze your chances for prosperity. Romans 13:8 states:

"Owe no man anything, but to love one another".
> ▶ *Determine* to get debt-free.
> ▶ *Study* the methods of others who have already achieved financial success.

100-Fold Return

Activate the principles of tithing and Seed-faith. Even the Pharisees were commended by Jesus for tithing (see Matthew 23:23). The best investment you can make is in God's work. Mark 10:29, 30 says: "And Jesus answered and said, Verily I say unto you, There is no man that hath left house, or brethren, or sisters, or father, or mother, or wife, or children, or lands, for My sake, and the gospel's, But he shall receive an hundredfold now in this time, houses, and brethren, and sisters, and mothers, and children, and lands, with persecutions; and in the world to come eternal life".

God guaranteed abundance in Malachi 3, as the resulting rewards for obedience for sowing our finances into His work. Start giving *regularly, liberally with expectation!* The *amount* and *attitude* determine your Harvest.

> ▶ "Give, and it shall be given unto you; good measure, pressed down, and shaken together, and running over, shall men give into your bosom. For with the same measure that ye mete withal it shall be measured to you again" (Luke 6:38).
> ▶ "But this I say, he which soweth sparingly shall reap also sparingly; and he which soweth bountifully shall reap also bountifully" (2 Corinthians 9:6).

LIE 8: *Regularity of giving and amount of your Seed does not really matter to God.*

Wrong. Inconsistent, erratic giving does not produce a consistent Harvest. The successful farmer depends on the regularity of evolving seasons, not momentary feelings: "Upon the first day of the week let every one of you lay by him in store, as God hath prospered him," (1 Corinthians 16:2). Whether weekly or monthly, establish the success *pattern* of consistent giving to your home church and various ministries that bless you.

Jesus noted the size of offerings (see Mark 12:42-44). He respected "sacrificial giving"; doing without temporal things temporarily, to secure the eternal benefits. The attitude is revealed by the amount we keep for ourselves, and that which is given back to God: "Every man according as he purposeth in his heart, so let him give; not grudgingly, or of necessity: for God loveth a cheerful giver" (2 Corinthians 9:7).

LIE 9: *Money is an unspiritual subject and not to be discussed in church.*

Ridiculous! The Bible is filled with warnings and promises regarding riches and wealth.
- ▶ *Money lovers* must be *warned.*
- ▶ The *giver* should be *encouraged.*
- ▶ Money is a major part of our daily life. The minister is responsible for putting *balance* to its importance.
- ▶ *Offering time* in churches is *worship time.*
- ▶ *Offering time* is *investment time.*
- ▶ *Offering time* is a period of *ministering* unto God and to our own future.

▶ *Offering time* is a season of *thanksgiving* and *appreciation*.

A Personal Word To Ministers

Oh, my minister friend, take time to *inform* your people of the Principles of Blessing in God's Word! How else will they know? Do not let a cynical sinner or critical church member limit or dilute your revelation on financial blessing.

The Bible teaches it. God must assuredly value the *giving system*. Certainly offerings deserve more time than a three-minute "usher-rush" to the back of the church! Take time to *inform* your people. *Information breeds confidence*. And, they have a right to be a part of God's *reward-systems*.

LIE 10: *The lie that it is selfish and wrong to give expecting to receive more in return.*

Though this lie makes little sense, thousands believe it. Wearing the mask of false humility, a man approached me recently with a proud, Pharisee strut. "I think it is selfish to want something in return. When I give, I expect nothing back from God," he snorted. His blatant ignorance and desire to advertise it appalled me! I had to ask him three questions.

"When you gave your *life* to Christ, did you expect *forgiveness* in return?"

"Uh, yes," he replied nervously.

"Aha! Selfish, were you?" I responded.

"When you are *sick,* do you expect *healing?*"

"Yes," his reply was a bit slow.

"I see. Selfish streak there. Then when you

became a Christian, you gave God what *you* had, to get what *He* had for you? Peace of mind, inner joy?"

He began to grin sheepishly. "I see what you mean."

Oh, my friend, listen to me today! *Your expectation is faith.* Nothing pleasures your Father more. You see, the God-man relationship is based on *exchange.* Life itself is based on *exchange.*

God wants your heart. You want *His* peace.

God wants your will. You want *His* plan.

Deuteronomy 28 promises that your *obedience* will bring God's *blessing.* You give God what He wants, and in return He gives you the desires of your heart (see Deuteronomy 28:1,2).

If a father offers $5 to his son to wash the car, he does it to *motivate. It is not wrong for the son to wash the car to receive $5!* While the son acted in obedience to please his father, the money was the incentive.

Selfishness Versus Self-Care

Self-care is wanting something good for yourself. That is not evil. You want salvation. You want peace, success and victory for your life. God wants you to have it.

Selfishness is *depriving another to advantage yourself.* Selfish people willingly hurt others to get ahead. This is an abomination to God.

God placed a desire for *more* inside your heart. When it becomes distorted and magnified, it is destructive. When focused on God and His principles, it is the energy for your progress in life. Dare to reach up! Dare to grow! Dare to *expect* financial blessings as you share the gospel. *Jesus gave it for motivation* in Luke 6:38: "Give, and it shall be given unto you; good measure, pressed down,

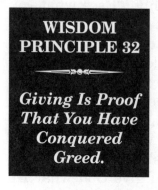

WISDOM PRINCIPLE 32

Giving Is Proof That You Have Conquered Greed.

and shaken together, and running over, shall men given into your bosom".

Your strongest desire should be to please your Father, *regardless* of the cost. The proof of your faith is in your *expectation* of *Harvest. Your release* determines your *increase.*

▶ *Giving is God's cure for greed.*

▶ It reveals your faith that He is your Provider.

▶ It shows you care about others.

▶ It is God's investment plan for His children. *And, it works!*

Perhaps your greatest problem is not financial, but spiritual or physical. God's laws of giving and receiving are effective in all areas. If you are lacking a relationship with God, *you must give in order to receive.* Give your heart, mind, soul and spirit! Let go of your past failures, sins, guilt. *Receive* Jesus as Lord, eternal life, healing for your disease, financial prosperity and forgiveness! Receive now the mentality of a victorious and successful *Winner!*

RECOMMENDED BOOKS:

B-82 31 Reasons People Do Not Receive Their Financial Harvest
(229 pages/$12)

⪦ 10 ⪧

GREED, GOLD AND GIVING

The World Is Running Scared.

Fear is eating the insides of Americans like a cancerous sore. In the middle of it, financial disaster threatens the heart of the economy: inflation, job losses, soaring prices, unbelievable interest rates.

3 Facts To Consider

1. **The Power Of Gold.**
2. **The Problem Of Greed.**
3. **The Promises Through Giving.**

What lies behind the mysterious power of gold, money, financial wealth? What makes it the human measure for worth? What is the magnetism of riches?

The natural instinct of man for self-preservation becomes an obsession. The need to dominate, to control, to own is an effort to establish a sense of importance, a sense of self-worth. We buy property. We fence it in. The *"ownership obsession"* can warp our sense of values. James 2:1-9 implies that wealthy persons should not receive special attention and favor. So, to God, wealth is hardly a measure of true worth.

Two extreme views exist regarding prosperity.

1. That Money Is The Essence Of Life.

However, Jesus said: "...beware of covetousness: for

a man's life consisteth not in the abundance of the things which he possesseth" (Luke 12:15).

2. **That Money Is *Unimportant.*** Yet, the responsibility of providing for a family (see 1 Timothy 5:8), and of supporting ministers (see Romans 10:14,15) is only possible through the financial blessing God promised in Malachi and Deuteronomy.

Gold has the power to build churches, hospitals, and send missionaries around the world. Yet, money can also become a *curse* (see 1 Timothy 6:9) or a *blessing* (see Proverbs 3:9,10).

Greed is the non-Christian's response to blessing. By scheming, stealing and sneaking, he hoards what should be shared.

God often permits the greedy person to accumulate, but withholds from his heart the *satisfaction* available to believers (see Ecclesiastes 4:8). God guarantees his *eventual failure* (see Proverbs 11:28) and a sense of *insecurity* (see Proverbs 23:5).

If gold is important for achievements, and greed becomes a major problem, why does God enjoy imparting wealth to people? If riches can be dangerous, why did He motivate us with promises of such wealth (see Deuteronomy 8:18)?

Think about this. Though fire destroys homes, when *properly* used, it cooks food, runs automobiles and warms homes. Though water drowns, it is *necessary* for life, for cleanliness and the beauty of a world. *Such is the use of gold.*

Giving is God's cure for greed.

The major difference between satan and God is that satan is a *taker* and *God is a giver.*

Satan *takes* joy, peace, love.

God *gives* joy, peace, love. Jesus said, "I am come that they might have life, and that they might have it more abundantly" (John 10:10). *Jesus was a Giver.* Of life. Of health. Of love. "For God so loved...that He GAVE" (John 3:16).

Therefore, giving is a God-characteristic.

Giving also impresses God (see Proverbs 3:9,10). God interprets an offering as a public honoring of Himself. To God, *an offering is faith in action.* So, *the danger of greed is solved through the act of giving.*

The need and importance of money is not ignored: *God promises response to our giving.* "Give, and it shall be given unto you; good measure, pressed down, and shaken together, and running over, shall men give into your bosom. For with the same measure that ye mete withal it shall be measured to you again" (Luke 6:38). "Bring ye all the tithes into the storehouse, that there may be meat in Mine house, and prove Me now herewith, saith the Lord of hosts, if I will not open you the windows of heaven, and pour you out a blessing, that there shall not be room enough to receive it. And I will rebuke the devourer for your sakes, and he shall not destroy the fruits of your ground; neither shall your vine cast her fruit before the time in the field, saith the Lord of hosts" (Malachi 3:10,11).

Why? *God always reacts to faith.*

Jesus marveled at faith.

> **WISDOM PRINCIPLE 33**
>
> ⇒►◄⇐
>
> *When You Let Go Of What Is In Your Hand, God Will Let Go Of What Is In His Hand For You.*

It impresses all of Heaven!

Giving an offering is an eternal proof of your internal faith (see Malachi 3:10,11)! When you sow your Seeds into God's work, your offering is evidence that you have:

▶ A *generous* heart (willingness to *share*).

▶ A *thankful* heart (willingness to *remember*).

▶ A *faith-filled* heart (willingness to *trust*).

▶ A *confident* heart (willingness to *expect*).

▶ *Your money represents you.* It is your time, your sweat, your energy, your mental abilities, your toil—a major part of you.

It is the *power* part of *you*. With it, you bargain—exchange your way through life. You trade it for food. For shelter. For clothing. You talk with your money. You tell your children you care through your providing.

When you give it to God, it is a public expression that He is important to you. He knows that. You release your money. That's faith in *Him*. That indicates your confidence in *Him*. You activate an *exchange* principle:

▶ You give your *sins* to Him...He gives *forgiveness* (see 1 John 1:9).

▶ You give your *confused mind*...He gives you *peace of mind* (see John 14:27).

▶ You give your *unclean heart*...He gives you a *new one* (see Ezekiel 36:26).

▶ You *release what you have*...and He *releases what He has for you.*

Your giving is your *love in action*.

It is the *power principle of total prosperity*.

≈ 11 ≈

THE LOVE FACTOR IN GIVING

"Mike, do you know what I need more than anything in this world? I need *love*."

I looked at my friend. He was wearing expensive jewelry and an impeccable suit, yet his face was etched with the pain of his recent divorce. I understood his loneliness completely. But I had to disagree.

"Friend, you are swamped with people who love you. You hardly need another name to add to your list. What you are needing is someone to *give* your love to."

Your need to give is as strong as your need to receive.

The world cries, "I need love!"

Jesus commanded, "*Give* love."

This is my fascination with Jesus Christ: *the love factor.* It astounded the Roman mentality of the first century. The armies of man accustomed to *force* found the power of *favor* beyond their understanding.

That is one of the reasons Christmas is important to Christians; not mere trees, toys and candy. We celebrate Christmas because of the love factor. We *give* gifts at Christmas because *giving* is the proof of love.

> ▶ "For God so loved...that He gave" (John 3:16).
> ▶ "...Christ also loved the church, and gave Himself for it" (Ephesians 5:25).

The love factor confuses the non-Christian who equates *love* with *approval*. The sinner cannot grasp that Jesus loves the *unqualified*. The very moment he truly embraces this truth, he will gladly commit his entire life to Jesus Christ.

> ▶ *Love* is the *attitude; giving* is the resulting *action*.
> ▶ *Love* is *the placement of value on another.*
> ▶ *Giving* is *depriving yourself in order to benefit another.*

I love Christmas. Quite frankly, I get excited about reading notes from my friends inside the special cards, and I've still got enough "kid" in me to love opening surprise packages and presents.

But there is more to Christmas than trees and lights. Christmas is a *celebration of love*, the nature of God.

And, His love is perpetuated through giving.

6 Principles Of Giving

1.   **Giving Is A God Characteristic.** "...how much more shall your Father which is in heaven give good things to them that ask Him?" (Matthew 7:11).

2.   **Godly Giving Is To Express Our Appreciation.** "A gift is as a precious stone in the eyes of him that hath it:" (Proverbs 17:8).

3.   **Everyone Has A Need To Give.** "...freely ye have received, freely give" (Matthew 10:8).

4.   Everyone Has Something To Give. "As every man hath received the gift, even so minister the same one to another," (1 Peter 4:10). It may be a spoken word of *thanks,* a small bouquet of *flowers,* an hour of *time,* a bag of *groceries,* a *commendation* for a job well done, use of your special gift or *ability.* Don't give what you don't have—*give what you have.*

5.   Do Not Let Rejection Of Your Gift Stop Your Continued Giving. Jesus kept giving though "...His own received Him not" (John 1:11). Your gift may be rejected if: 1) It is not *really needed;* 2) It is not *valued'*; 3) Its' purpose is not *discerned.*

6.   God Treasures The Giver. He sees His own nature in you and honors it with the *promise of prosperity:* "Give, and it shall be given unto you; good measure, pressed down, and shaken together, and running over, shall men give into your bosom. For with the same measure that you mete withal it shall be measured to you again" (Luke 6:38).

Sow with great expectation today.

Your Uncommon Seed Will Always Create An Uncommon Harvest.

WISDOM PRINCIPLE 34

When What You Hold In Your Hand Is Not Enough To Be A Harvest, Make It A Seed.

Money Is Simply
A Reward
For Solving A Problem.

-*MIKE MURDOCK*

❧ 12 ❧

THE LAW OF RELEASE

Only fools do not want to *grow*...to *add*...to *gain*...to *increase.* In fact, there is a parable in which Jesus said He looked to see if the servants were *gaining* (see Matthew 25:14-30).

The Law Of Growth Is A Law Of Life

If your child still weighed nine pounds at five years of age, you would know something was wrong. There are Christians who never grow. Something is out of order. Some simply have never learned the importance of personal *growth*...increase... enlarging...prospering.

WISDOM PRINCIPLE 35

Your Seed Is Like A Purchase Order In The Warehouse Of Heaven... Authorizing Miracle Packages To Be Sent Into Your Life.

What about *you?* Do you want to grow?

God planned on your increase.

I can look in the Scriptures (Deuteronomy 8:18; Deuteronomy 28:1-14; Malachi 3:9-11; Luke 6:38; Proverbs 3;) and know quickly that God *does* take pleasure in the *prosperity* of His people! "Praise ye the Lord. Blessed is the man that feareth the Lord, that delighteth greatly in His commandments. His Seed shall be mighty upon earth: the generation of the upright shall be blessed. Wealth and riches shall be in his house: and his righteousness endureth for ever" (Psalm 112:1-3).

I hardly need to take the time to prove that to anyone. *Abundance* is an important *key* in enjoying the winning life—abundance of *energy,* abundance of *health,* abundance of *Wisdom,* abundance of *friends* and an abundance of *favor.*

Most people want to grow financially. Even teenagers want "more." Parents love their children and want to provide them with a good education, good books and a comfortable home. You are God's child. If something interests you—then God is interested. What activates your increase? What starts the avalanche of blessing?

The Law of R-E-L-E-A-S-E.

The farmer never sees the harvest of corn until he *releases the seed* into the ground. You must *let go* of what you have before God can release what He has. *Release* is the action of faith.

Releasing says, "I believe God."

Releasing says, "It is possible to see my miracle."

Releasing says, "I am master of my finances... money does not control me."

Releasing says, "God is more important than the money I have in my bank account."

Releasing is proof that you are not a lover or a hoarder of finances. (In fact, there is no better way of proving that you are not a money lover than through your demonstration of *releasing*!!)

Jesus saw the widow woman who gave her "mite." *All she had.* God saw the widow who gave the cake to Elijah. The Lord blessed *both* with an *increase*.

4 Miracles Of Releasing

1. **When You Release, You Open The Very Floodgates Of Heaven.**
2. **When You Release, You Demonstrate Your Love For God.**
3. **When You Release, You Should Begin Expecting The Miraculous Provision Of God.**
4. **When You Release What You Have— Time, Talent, Finances, Love—It Will Come Back To You.**

It will come back to you! I really believe that! *Start looking for the Harvest!* If you have not planted Seeds, start doing so. As you give, expect God's absolute *best*.

Stop complaining about lack and expect *plenty* from God. You are a *Winner*. You are operating within the *Laws of Increase*. You are activating the *Law of Increase*, by *practicing the Law of Release*.

Let go! Let go! Take your hands off of what you think is *yours*, and admit it: "God, it is *yours!* I release it to *you!*"

When you give to God, what you hold in your hand, He gives to you, what He holds in His hand.

Now...get excited! *You have just stepped into the Winning Life.*

When Satan Wants
    To Destroy You
He Sends A Person
    Into Your Life.

-MIKE MURDOCK

⮩ 13 ⮨

HOW TO ACHIEVE
HAPPINESS ON YOUR JOB

Is your present job a drudgery or delight?

Being on the proper job and in the right career is an important key for *total* happiness. Some blame families, their mate, their children for their frustrations, when the truth would reveal that job unhappiness is "eating them up" inside.

Your work is supposed to be a source of joy! "To rejoice in his labour; this is the gift of God" (Ecclesiastes 5:19). "Mine elect shall long enjoy the work of their hands" (Isaiah 65:22). "The Lord shall command the blessing upon thee...and in all that thou settest thine hand unto;" (Deuteronomy 28:8).

Your business is very important. It provides a sense of accomplishment that is essential for self-esteem. It *releases* your God-given *talents.* It *provides* for your family.

That's why one of satan's goals is to destroy your self-confidence and your sense of worth. A feeling of inadequacy can be the "cancer" that eats away your vitality and enthusiasm.

Are you unhappy with your job? Why? Is it conflict with another person? Is it lack of personal skills to do the job right? Are your God-given abilities being used *now?* Is it a "waiting room" for *eventual* promotion?

▶ *You may be on the right job presently but en route to something more suitable.* Your present job could be a "temporary training ground." So, stay steady. Don't ruin friendships and your reputation through an outburst of anger or frustration. *Wait.* Do your best "as unto the Lord."

▶ *You may be on the wrong job.* Are you happy with what you are doing? Is God happy with your present work? Do you work as if God is your "boss?" Are you really giving your *best?* Be honest with yourself and do something about it! (You may want to order a copy of my powerful booklet, "Four Forces That Guarantee Career Success." It is only $5.00. It could change your life.)

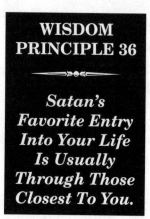

WISDOM PRINCIPLE 36

Satan's Favorite Entry Into Your Life Is Usually Through Those Closest To You.

▶ *Those who are faithful in the little things advance to greater.* Ephesians 6:5 and 8 says: "Servants,be obedient to them that are your masters...Knowing that whatsoever good thing any man doeth, the same shall he receive of the Lord."

8 Facts You Should Know About Work

1.   **Work Began In The Garden Of Eden.** Adam was to dress the garden and keep it (see Genesis 2:15). This work was an activity blessed of the Lord to provide Adam with a sense of achievement and self-worth.

Then Adam sinned. His disobedience turned work into a curse: "In the sweat of thy face shalt thou eat bread, till thou return unto the ground; for out of it wast thou taken: for dust thou art, and unto dust shalt thou return" (Genesis 3:19).

2. Obedience To The Laws Of God Can Reinstate The Blessings Of Work. Deuteronomy 28:8 states: "The Lord shall command the blessing upon thee in thy storehouses, and in all that thou settest thine hand unto." Many despise their jobs. Husbands lash out at their wives in frustration. Many wives arrive home work-weary and angered at the expectations of the family to "keep on working" after they get home.

3. If You Are Unhappy At Work, It Will Affect Your Family Life, Even Your Health. Take time to plan your career and life's work. It deserves *your* attention. Do not accept a job based simply on convenient location or financial sufficiency or even friendship.

4. Find What You Are Good At And Do It With All Your Heart. Be proud of what you are involved in. Never "put down" your occupation. See and cultivate an awareness of its important place in the lives of people. Strive to be the best you can be: "For which of you, intending to build a tower, sitteth not down first, and counteth the cost, whether he have sufficient to finish it?" (Luke 14:28).

5. You Must Learn To Conquer Conflict On The Job. One of the frustrations people face on their jobs is *people-conflict*. Anger, hostility and open resentment have caused some to leave their jobs prematurely. God has really touched my spirit in this area. As a minister, many times I am in a "controlled" climate. Since I am with fellow Christians and many other top quality people most of the time, it is sometimes easy to forget the intense pressure many husbands and wives face on the everyday job.

6. Conflict With Your Boss May Be Caused By Different Reasons. He may be having personal problems at home and is trying to compensate through job productivity. He may be experiencing the pressure of a power struggle from within the organization. He may be suppressing hostility stemming from an attitude he has discerned in you. *Talk travels!* Have you shown a rebellious attitude or expressed it to another? Do you follow his instructions? Does he continually find it necessary to repeat his instructions to you?

7. Misunderstandings Occur When The Details Of A Job Are Not Clearly Defined. Take the time to grasp clearly what your boss or employees expect. Take nothing for granted. Aim for *quality* in your work production.

8. Remember That God Is Your True Employer. "With good will doing service, as to the Lord, and not to men:" (Ephesians 6:7).

20 Keys For Winning At Work

Happiness depends on feeling good about yourself. It is based on your relationships and achievements. When your gifts and abilities are developed and utilized through your life's work, you grow in confidence and strength.

There are *keys* with which you can *unlock* the treasures of accomplishment and confidence in your work.

1. Accept Work As God's Gift, Not Punishment. "...to rejoice in his labour; this is the gift of God" (Ecclesiastes 5:19; also see Deuteronomy 28:1-14).

2. Recognize God As Your True Employer. "With good will doing service, as to the Lord, and not to men" (Ephesians 6:7).

3. Pursue Work Compatible With Your Abilities And Interests. "Neglect not the gift that is in thee" (1 Timothy 4:14), Paul encouraged Timothy (see 2 Timothy 4:5; also see Ephesians 4:11). Solomon also recognized skills (see 2 Chronicles 2:7-14).

4. Learn Everything Possible About Your Job. "...give attendance to reading" (1 Timothy 4:13). "A wise man will hear, and will increase learning" (Proverbs 1:5).

5. Don't Be A Time Thief. "Redeeming the time, because the days are evil" (Ephesians 5:16). "Let him that stole steal no more: but rather let him labour, working with his hands the thing which is good, that he may have to give to him that needeth" (Ephesians 4:28).

6. Keep A Daily Master List Of Priorities And Establish Reasonable Deadlines. "...this one thing I do" (Philippians 3:13). "To every thing there is a season" (Ecclesiastes 3:1).

7. Ask The Holy Spirit For Wisdom During Decision-Making. "If any of you lack wisdom, let him ask of God, that giveth to all men liberally, and upbraideth not; and it shall be given him" (James 1:5).

8. Use All Criticism To Your Advantage.

In fact, get on the positive side of it: *Ask* your boss for suggestions and correction: "Poverty and shame shall be to him that refuseth instruction: but he that regardeth reproof shall be honoured" (Proverbs 13:18).

9. Be Swift To Admit Your Mistakes. "He that covereth his sins shall not prosper: but whoso confesseth and forsaketh them shall have mercy" (Proverbs 28:13).

10. Be Quick To Ask For Assistance And Necessary Information When Needed. "...a man of knowledge increaseth strength...in multitude of counsellors there is safety" (Proverbs 24:5,6).

11. Assist Others In Their Responsibilities When Possible. "Withhold not good from them to whom it is due, when it is in the power of thine hand to do it" (Proverbs 3:27).

12. Project The Nature Of Jesus In Genuine Love And Enthusiasm. Resist the *"Holier-than-thou"* attitude: "...the servant of the Lord must not strive; but be gentle unto all men, apt to teach, patient" (2 Timothy 2:24).

13. Do Not Receive Nor Repeat Gossip. "Speak not evil one of another" (James 4:11). "He that covereth a transgression seeketh love; but he that repeateth a matter separateth very friends" (Proverbs 17:9). "The words of a talebearer are as wounds" (Proverbs 26:22). "Whoso keepeth his mouth and his tongue keepeth his soul from

> **WISDOM PRINCIPLE 37**
>
> ─►●◄─
>
> *Confidentiality Is One Of The Most Treasured Gifts You Can Give To Another.*

troubles" (Proverbs 21:23).

14. Insist On Giving Others A Second Chance. "But the wisdom that is from above is first pure...full of mercy" (James 3:17). "Blessed are the merciful: for they shall obtain mercy" (Matthew 5:7).

15. Do More Than Your Boss Expects You To Do. "And whosoever shall compel thee to go a mile, go with him twain" (Matthew 5:41).

16. Refocus Your Anger Toward A Realistic Change. "He that hath no rule over his own spirit is like a city that is broken down, and without walls" (Proverbs 25:28). "He that is soon angry dealeth foolishly" (Proverbs 14:17). "He that is slow to anger is better than the mighty; and he that ruleth his spirit than he that taketh a city" (Proverbs 16:32).

17. Keep Accurate Records, Including Receipts For Everything. "Be thou diligent to know the state of thy flocks, and look well to thy herds" (Proverbs 27:23).

18. Refuse To Give Or Receive Unearned Adulation. "As he that bindeth a stone in a sling, so is he that giveth honour to a fool" (Proverbs 26:8). "...a flattering mouth worketh ruin" (Proverbs 26:28).

19. Never Yield To Bribery, Intimidation Or Coercion. "A wicked man taketh a gift out of the bosom to pervert the ways of judgment" (Proverbs 17:23). "Be not afraid of their faces: for I am with thee to deliver thee, said the Lord" (Jeremiah 1:8).

20. Focus On Pleasing Only The Holy Spirit. Keep conscious of the Holy Spirit throughout the day as you do your duties faithfully. "Thou wilt keep him in perfect peace, whose mind is stayed on Thee: because he trusteth in Thee" (Isaiah 26:3).

Home Should Be
The Nest
Without Thorns.

-MIKE MURDOCK

❧ 14 ❧
TWENTY KEYS TO A BETTER MARRIAGE

Nothing feels better than a good marriage.
Nothing hurts worse than an unhappy one.

Someone has said that the home can be like Heaven or like hell. Your home and marriage affects you more than anything else. A man can have an old car and still enjoy life. A woman can live in a small, cramped apartment and still be glad she is married. But when the marriage is crumbling, there is nothing else to fill that particular "emptiness." God created man for a mate (see Genesis 2:18).

What are some of the *keys* to a better marriage? There are hundreds of suggestions from everywhere. In my office, as I write this, my shelves are filled with books about marriage, the home, and the husband's and wife's expectations of each other. One husband writes as though the cure-all in a marriage is to bring roses every week to his wife or wash the dishes for her. One wife thinks all the husband really wants is for her to be beautiful and sensuous when he comes home from work.

It can be a bit ridiculous. Personally, I don't think what works with one marriage will necessarily work for another. All of us have *different needs* at *different times and stages* in our lives.

The 20 Success Keys I have included here are

things to observe as you look at your marriage through the eyes of God. Remember: Success is achieving the goals *God* has for you. You know that His goal for you is a good marriage.

The *Golden Key to Success is Understanding*— which is the ability to interpret a situation or person as God does. A marvelous miracle would be to see your wife or husband as *God* sees them today.

20 Success Keys To A Better Marriage

1.   Recognize The Value God Places On Your Marriage. If marriage was not a powerful tool for your success in other areas of your life, God would not have ordained it. Do you truly *value* your family life? God does. He knew it would affect your relationships with other people (see Genesis 2:18).

2.   Recognize That Satan Hates A Good Marriage. A good marriage is a powerful force against evil. In a good marriage, a husband and wife will strengthen one another for God. They will teach their children how to discern between good and evil.

3.   Discern Undesirable Influences And Protect Yourself From Them. Do you have certain friends that have an unsettling effect on your home life? One woman noticed her marriage pressures were not nearly so great when a particular friend left town or went on vacation, so she limited her time spent with that person (see 1 Corinthians 15:33).

4.   Rebuild Good Influences Into Your Home Climate. Christian music and Christian friends should be brought into your home circle frequently. Good books should be picked up regularly for the family to read. Christian bookstores are everywhere. *Take advantage of your local bookstore.* I thank God for my own parents who constantly bought books, records and tapes for me over the years. They influenced me greatly. They took me to youth rallies and youth camps. They continually looked for ways to expose my heart to the climate of God.

5. Make Church The Center Of Family Activities. Make it the hub of life. If there must be a limitation in your activities, let it be the job or school, but never the church life. Let your pastor be an important man in your home life. If Bible questions arise, let it be a natural thing to consult church leaders who are "mentoring" your family.

6. Respect The Opinions Of Others In Your Home And Prove It By Asking Worthwhile Questions And Listening To The Answers. All of us crave respect. We want to feel we count—that what we say *will* matter! Obviously, we cannot follow all the advice given, but sometimes just merely considering it will be of tremendous value. Respect the *privacy* of other family members. Respect *their* time.

7. Discern The Favorable Qualities In Your Mate. Notice what others like about your mate and *verbalize* it. If others enjoy your mate, why do you focus on the things you do not like? Ask your friends and notice the qualities *they* admire—then express those qualities to your mate: "I really appreciate the time you spend at work making us a living." "You keep a clean house!" Their significance can be found through focusing on their *strengths*, not their *weaknesses*.

8. Use The Irritating Qualities Of Your

Mate As A Stepping Stone To A Higher Spiritual Goal In Your Life. Let them be like "sandpaper" removing your rough edges. Patience can be built into your life. God is allowing them as a test to your life. Do not run from them. *Develop...grow... mature...*through their pressure on you!

9. **Establish A Family Altar Time.** I will not pretend this is easy. It is *not,* but it is possible and unbelievably powerful. I remember when I saw my own parents reading the Bible and praying. I thought subconsciously: "This must be important. God must really talk to them." Most children will not rebel nearly as much when they see and hear their parents praying and reading the Word. I think wives who see their husbands disciplined in this way are most apt to respect them as the Scriptures teach.

10. **Take Authority Over Every Attack Of Satan In Your Home.** Learn to recognize satanic attacks upon your family and use your authority as a born-again Christian, and child of the King. You can take control of satan by the very name of Jesus. This is your privilege as a believer.

11. **Minimize The Problem Areas Of Your Marriage.** Everyone has them. Some just know how to "play the rough edges down." Don't talk to just anybody and everybody about your private problems.

12. **Focus At Least Once A Week On The Possibilities Of Your Mate, Not The Problems.** This is definitely not easy. But *try it!* Help your mate to develop a good *self-image.*

13. **Talk Faith-Talk In Your Home.** Do not allow talk of doubt about everything in your house. When someone starts talking about the bad weather,

another of how he dreads to go to school, another about the new boss who is not nice—such talk will affect the climate and atmosphere of your home! *Stop it!* Talk about the *blessings* of God, the *good* things that are happening. Never talk "divorce." Do not pave the road to failure. Do not make it easy for yourself to slip and slide. If divorce is never talked, it probably won't be as easy to do (see James 3:2).

14. Work Toward Financial Freedom Not Accumulation. *Possessions* will become *pressures* if they are not acquired on God's *timing.* If too many purchases are made, the appreciation level is usually much lower and short-lived.

15. Assign And Require Accountability For Household Responsibilities. Most people are not strongly self-motivated. Do not expect more than family members are capable of. Homes that have clear and defined responsibilities for each child and parent are free from confusion.

16. Keep Confidences And Respect Privacy. I think sometimes home is where we learn distrust instead of trust. Husband and wife should not betray each other's confidence in front of the children. Neither should they expose one child's inner world to another. *Confidentiality is one of the most treasured gifts you can give to another.* To me, discretion is more than evidence of Wisdom, it is the *proof of love.*

17. Pray For Specific Ways To Meet The Needs Of Those In Your Family. You may be their *only key* to inner happiness. Let God give you the proper "burden and compassion" for those around you.

18. Refuse To Grieve The Holy Spirit.

Maintain an inner relationship with God. Learn to pray often *in the language of the Holy Spirit.* Constantly build yourself and edify yourself in the Holy Spirit.

19. Schedule Play Time. This is just as important as any other part of your life. Enjoy life together, have fun in each other's company. God ordained the family for your pleasure.

20. Never Give Up. Keep trying to make your home a happy place. Review these 20 Keys continuously. There will always be crisis experiences. There will always be times of setbacks. *Minimize them and maximize the good times.*

Our Children And Their Success

1. Children Listen.

Children *observe.* They *absorb.* They are like "containers"—in their ears we deposit faith or fear, victory or defeat, motivation or depression. Unfortunately, in their early years they are unable to push the "reject" button when error is introduced.

When the disciples rebuked children, Jesus said, *"...Suffer little children, and forbid them not to come unto Me: for of such is the kingdom of heaven"* (Matthew 19:14).

At eight years of age, after my minister father finished preaching, I walked to an altar in Waco, Texas, and publicly committed my life to Jesus Christ. *I still remember the experience.* I felt something stir inside me and it still exists today.

What are your children hearing? My father has never allowed a television in his home...nor cursing ...nor screaming. Strict? Perhaps, but he knew the *influence* of what we *heard.* Instead, we heard him and my mother weeping and praying daily for our salvation and understanding of truth. The difference has been permanently engraved upon my heart.

2. Children Learn.

Through you, your children learn to laugh or criticize, rebel or cooperate, take or give.

You stand at their crossroads. You are their signpost. *You* are their *source of education* in spiritual things.

The mentality of the unbelieving dad still stuns me. How can a man hug his child and say "I love you"—then never help that child serve Christ, but *watch him go to hell?*

Tragic ignorance. "But whoso shall offend one of these little ones which believe in Me, it were better for him that a millstone were hanged about his neck, and that he were drowned in the depth of the sea" (Matthew 18:6).

3. Children Lean.

Youth *long* for a sign of *strength.* They will test every emotional fiber of a parent. In the midst of an inner roller coaster, they are searching for a *rock.* Sometimes they even panic in their search.

Mom and dad, your children need you. They may not say it. They may not *know* it. But stand strong. They want to see you *win* in adversity. *You may be the only visible source of faith they have.* Please don't destroy that.

They lean on *your* Wisdom, *your* experience with God. They lean on you for affection and love. *Give it.* Resist those awkward feelings and dare to *reach* out to your family. "He that troubleth his own house shall inherit the wind:" (Proverbs 11:29).

Your home and family are irreplaceable.

Don't Poison
    Your Future
With The Pain
    Of The Past.

-Mike Murdock

～ 15 ～

DEALING WITH THE TRAGEDY OF DIVORCE

It has been said that divorce is the greatest *emotional* pain that the human heart can experience.

I believe it.

It destroys the *sense of worth* we desperately crave. It has brought heartache to millions. The scars are carried for a lifetime. My purpose in this chapter is not to multiply the memories, or magnify the scars, nor to condemn. My purpose is to heal, to strengthen, to restore purpose and to aid in total recovery.

Jesus knew the intense pain divorce could bring. "For this cause shall a man leave his father and mother, and cleave to his wife; And they twain shall be one flesh; so then they are no more twain, but one flesh. What therefore God hath joined together, let not man put asunder" (Mark 10:7-9).

Many divorced people write to me every week asking whether they are "living in sin,"...or whether they will have committed the "unpardonable sin" if they should remarry after divorce. Too many times ministers tend to either compromise or condemn because of lack of sufficient information, past prejudiced teaching or inexperience.

It often seems that those who *cause* the divorce

rarely seek help. Seldom do they search for solid answers, consult consistently with counselors, nor do they assume personal responsibility for their conflicts. Yet, these people are almost always the *only* targets of the sermons preached to the divorced! The *victim* of divorce is often ignored and many times treated like the one who *caused* the divorce! It is like the *raped,* instead of the rapist, *being brought to trial!* For that reason, I want to focus on how to keep a *winning* attitude even when the stigma of divorce has touched your life.

At the age of 32, I had experienced a measure of success as a young evangelist who had traveled in more than 30 countries in crusades. I had been married for thirteen years and loved it. Quite frankly, I was quite critical of those who had unhappy marriages. Something was wrong with their personalities, I reasoned, or they really didn't try very hard, or they simply didn't exercise enough "positive thinking" and faith in God!

Then, suddenly, it happened to me. I was faced with a situation that was overwhelming. My emotions "went crazy." One minute I was full of faith; the next moment fear would seize my heart. I saw a lifetime of dreams evaporate before my very eyes.

And I felt totally helpless.

Of course, everyone around had good answers. (They had the same answers I had before I was *"there!"* It's always easier to tell the next man how to swim when you are not in the water with him!)

Oh, I knew God. I knew the *principles* taught in the Scriptures. I had spent years studying total success and victorious living.

But, I felt like an utter failure. It seemed that

everything I had believed, lived and tried to teach had backfired. There was only one thing I knew to do...*stay connected to God.*

And somehow I did.

I might add, God does restore. Over 5,700 songs have been written from the various pages of that experience. Songs such as, "You Can Make It," "I Am Blessed," "God's Not Through Blessing You," and many others. I value God more than ever before. And I have cultivated more *discerning* to sense integrity, character and honesty. Oh, yes, and I've learned to *release* hostility, anger and bitterness *out* of my life.

I would like to share part of my experience with you. First, I found *me* blaming myself, Mike Murdock, for every single failure I could recall in my life! My thoughts were on *past* circumstances instead of *future* challenges! Everything I had ever done wrong was reprogrammed into my daily "diet of memories."

I chewed, and chewed, and re-chewed old memories until I discovered the reason God gave us Isaiah 43:18,19: "Remember ye not the former things, neither consider the things of old. Behold, I will do a new thing; now it shall spring forth; shall ye not know it? I will even make a way in the wilderness, and rivers in the desert." *God gave me the power to break a mind-fixation on the past,* and increased my ability to picture the

WISDOM PRINCIPLE 38

—————

Stop Looking At Where You Have Been And Begin Looking At Where You Are Going.

"blessings of tomorrow."

Have you been crushed by someone you *totally trusted?* Have you felt *devastated* and *ruined?* Are you overwhelmed by loneliness in *the midnight hours?* Do you feel as though your hands are completely tied? Does it anger you to see friends *lacking* understanding?

▶ *Do not become weary.*

▶ *Your present circumstances will change.*

▶ *You will rebuild.* You will *grow.* You will not *stay* down.

▶ *You will win again.*

▶ *It will take a little time.*

▶ *You will have to invest some effort.* And you may experience some pages of darkness in your "Diary of Success." But, you will start enjoying life *again,* loving *again* and learn the *real* secrets of inner power and peace.

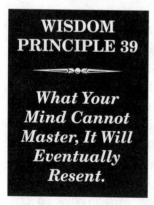

WISDOM PRINCIPLE 39

What Your Mind Cannot Master, It Will Eventually Resent.

Elizabeth Kübler-Ross, who did much work on how persons deal with the process of dying, discovered that many people process through five stages. I recognized these stages as descriptive of my own emotions following the breakup of my marriage.

1. The Stage Of Denial.

This is when we ignore or minimize what has happened to our marriage and home in hopes that it will just go away. We fear confrontation and refuse to face it. This is why many marriages fail. We won't go for help in hopes it will all just "work out in the end."

2. The Stage Of Anger.

What we do not understand, we fear.

What we fear, we fight.

What we fight, we frag-ment and destroy.

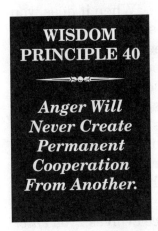

WISDOM PRINCIPLE 40

Anger Will Never Create Permanent Cooperation From Another.

At this point, we make wild unchecked statements that are born out of emotional chaos such as "Good! I'm glad it's over! You just wait, I'll find someone who *really* loves me and appreciates me." *Divorce is a rejection.* Rejection means *devaluation.* Our self-confidence is attacked and *our defense is anger.*

3. The Stage Of Bargaining.

Anger will never create permanent cooperation from another. So, seeing the *futility* of anger, we deftly apply the technique of *bargaining,* or seeking a solution or compromise. We justify or use other means to find the ability to accept the tragedy of rejection, loss or failure.

4. The Stage Of Depression.

This happens at the most inappropriate times... special days, birthdays, anniversaries, at restaurants with friends, or at 2:00 a.m., when we just cannot go to sleep.

Depression is usually the result of introspection. The cure is to discipline our thoughts toward a goal in our future or to concentrate on helping *someone else* achieve a worthy goal. (Use memories for *ministering* to others, not meditation! It is impossible to *think wrong*...and *feel good* at the same time.)

5.   The Stage Of Acceptance.

Believe it or not, acceptance *can* and eventually

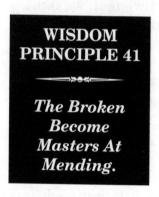

**WISDOM
PRINCIPLE 41**

*The Broken
Become
Masters At
Mending.*

does come. When it does, you will almost feel a tinge of guilt for not feeling depressed and sad! It does not come because you lose compassion or caring for those in your "past chapters" of living, but because the beauty of your days *ahead* becomes more evident. *You see recovery.* You taste the sweetness of new achievements. A climate of *peace* evolves...*you enter your future.*

At this point, I have experienced two additional stages relative to divorce:

6.   The Stage Of Hope.

Peace is a *present* need. Hope is the motivation for *tomorrow.* It says, "I will live and love again! My life is not over." *Purpose* is discovered. *Friendships* develop. You start growing rapidly. Emotionally, you age fast...and it becomes an *advantage.*

7.   The Stage Of Fulfillment.

Whether it is a *new* relationship, a new career or some particular achievement, God will see to it that you find fulfillment again. *Dare to believe that.* That is the place where complaining is never heard. Neither do we rehearse old memories of failure. We stop recycling our emotional "bandages" through the ears of friends. We are happier about tomorrow and

**WISDOM
PRINCIPLE 42**

*Don't Poison
Your Future
With The Pain
Of The Past.*

everyone knows it.

Now, I do not know what particular stage you are presently experiencing. But, I assure you, that *you can start winning again.*

You really can.

So, put your shoulders back. Hold your head up high. *Stop discussing* your moments of failure and start sharing your future successes, joys and triumphs. Your best days are *not* behind you, they are just *ahead.*

See it. *Feel* it. *Live* it.

What You Fail
    To Master
In Your Life
    Will Eventually
Master You.

-MIKE MURDOCK

☙ 16 ☙

HOW TO WIN OVER BITTERNESS

One of the most effective tools against sincere Christians is the tool of *bitterness*.

I do not recall my very first experience with a satanic attack of bitterness, but I have had enough throughout the years that I feel very qualified to speak about it.

Some years ago I knelt beside a man who was an ex-preacher. When I started talking to him about his soul, he looked up at me with an attitude of condescension: "Son, don't hand me those clichés. I've preached three times more than you have and to three times more people. I know all those scriptures that you are quoting to me. I simply can't get right with God. I'm *past feeling*."

I felt crushed. I looked at him with compassion. I did not recognize it at the time, but he was dying with a broken heart and *a spirit of bitterness*.

He explained. Some preachers had failed to stand by him during an attack upon his character. His wife had deserted him for another man. His children never telephoned him. He felt even church members were too busy gossiping to spend time helping an "ex-preacher." He *willingly* became a servant to bitterness.

Bitterness will make you a slave.

Bitterness will kill your spirit.

Bitterness will wipe the smile off your heart, and will sap and drain the river of blessing from your soul.

Bitterness will *paralyze your effectiveness* for God.

You must master bitterness or it will master you.

It happens to teenagers who trust someone and

WISDOM PRINCIPLE 43

What You Fail To Destroy, Will Eventually Destroy You.

are betrayed. It happens to parents who do all they know to do and still their children quit going to church. It happens to wives who try to follow the Scriptural pattern to lead their husbands to God, while they refuse to acknowledge the truth. Being ignored is tormenting. It can embitter.

Why I Almost Left The Ministry

I was almost destroyed some years back through bitterness. I was preaching for several ministers I had idolized for years since my youth. Large offerings were given to my ministry by the congregation. But when church leaders would often withhold half of my offerings for themselves, my heart literally broke. I was hardly given enough to pay my trailer note and car note, much less my house and living expenses. To my amazement, the coming weeks did not improve. The pattern continued to repeat itself during two months of meetings.

After eight weeks, I went into my trailer and

began to cry. For two solid hours I wept; not mad at God, but wounded toward people and preachers. I felt shoved to the side. *Mistreated.* Nobody cared about me. "Nobody cares," I spoke to a friend through heavy crying. "This is it. I am leaving the ministry. I don't have to put up with preachers and churches who don't care about my needs and family. I'm going into business. I will support the men I believe in, but God can have the rest of them!"

WISDOM PRINCIPLE 44

Depression Will Always Follow Any Decision To Avoid A Priority.

At that moment, satan and God were in combat. *My eyes were on people. I had made preachers, churches and people the source of my supply instead of God.* God was wanting to teach me a lesson.

I almost did not learn it.

To be honest with you, I did not see a vision. I saw no stars nor received any singing telegrams sung by angels at the foot of my bed. No man seven feet tall touched my shoulder, but in a matter of weeks, as the anointing of God oozed out of my spirit, I suddenly lost confidence and faith in people.

I lost my desire for the Word.

I did not want to pray. I literally lost my desire to live. Yet, I was still attempting to minister each night in the crusades, but harboring bitterness in my spirit.

I woke up one morning at 5:00 a.m. and the Spirit of God impressed me to pray. I stumbled into the sanctuary (I was staying in evangelist's quarters) and knelt down. Suddenly, my very soul erupted like a volcano. I gushed with tears (and I don't cry easily). God showed me I had let some friends *encourage* my bitterness. I had not looked at the *lesson* God wanted me to learn through the experience. God showed me my *disappointment and hurt* was because of my pride and doubt in His promises and provision.

God heard my cry for help.

Needless to say, the *spirit of joy* returned to my life, and my ministry. (On several occasions, I have had to return to that "Bethel" for a *second* touch.)

You can win over your experience with bitterness. The bitterness may come through a divorce that occurs. A sickness. The loss of a friend. A child who dies. A financial setback. Regardless of what happens to you, make up your mind to overcome it!

11 Steps For Overcoming Bitterness

1. **Admit That You Are Living With The Sin Of Bitterness In Your Heart.**
2. **Admit That It Is Wrong And Damaging To You.**
3. **Admit Your Own Mistakes.**
4. **Look For The Lessons The Spirit Wants To Teach You.**
5. **Do Not Talk Your Bitterness To Others.**
6. **Stay In Harmony With Godly Friends.**
7. **Soak Your Soul In The Scripture, Preferably The Psalm Of David As He Cried Unto The Lord.**
8. **Plan New Projects In Your Future.**

9.   **Think Ahead And Not Backwards.**

10.   **Discuss Everything With The Holy Spirit —Bitterness Will Literally Be "Choked Out" And Displaced.**

11.   **Study Winners In The Bible, Those Who Won Over Bitterness** (like Joseph toward his brothers).

Never allow the root of bitterness to rob you of the success and joy you can experience in the Winner's World!

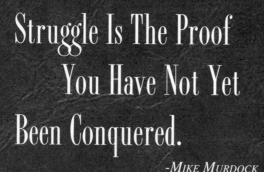

Struggle Is The Proof
You Have Not Yet
Been Conquered.

-*MIKE MURDOCK*

✎ 17 ✎

FIVE STEPS OUT OF DEPRESSION

———⟶●≪———

It was past midnight.

The crusade was over and I sat in an expensive home of the fine pastor of a very successful church. Two Cadillacs were parked in the drive. From *outward* appearance, life couldn't be better.

Yet, he was weeping.

"I have been in the ministry more than 20 years. God has blessed me more than I ever dreamed. Yet, I have been living with a depression that has brought me to the very brink of leaving the ministry. *It is like a wave about to drown me and my entire family.* What in the world is going wrong?"

Frankly, I had no pat answers. All I knew was that this scene was being repeated all too often in the ministry. *And if this was happening to clergymen, the leadership, what must be happening to our people?*

Certainly there are normal setbacks that motivate us to action. Temporary knocks that deflate our arrogance. But the depression in my minister friend was not the godly sorrow of 2 Corinthians 7:8-10 that "worketh repentance." It was the sorrow of disobedience that *worketh death.*

Your *motivation* is drained.

Your desire to *pursue* God is gone.

Your *conversations* become sour.
You are blinded to current blessings.
Your enthusiasm is *forced.*
You are in a daze regarding future plans.
You see *thorns* instead of *roses.*

There are *five steps* you can take out of such a state of mind. *There is a way out!* And it is a condition of the mind! *"...for as he thinketh in his heart, so is he:"* (Proverbs 23:7).

So, Paul encourages *thought-control.* "...whatsoever things are true...honest...just...pure... lovely...of good report...*think on these things"* (Philippians 4:8).

My father calls it, "The Whatsoever-Formula."

Your depression can be *temporary.* Our Heavenly Father will *"...give thee rest from thy sorrow,"* (Isaiah 14:3). Read on in faith! Regardless of how dark your circumstances, God's Word *"giveth light;"* (Psalm 119:130).

5 Steps Out Of Depression

1. Understand That Depression Can Come To Every One Of Us. Your feelings are not unique or unusual. Biographies of notables Abraham Lincoln and Winston Churchill record periods of great depression of these gifted personalities.

According to one survey by the National Institute of Mental Health, at any one time, perhaps one-third of the population is *experiencing* depression!

The Bible fascinates us with such details about the feelings of *highs* and *lows* of Spirit-filled men!

DAVID, a musician and king, sobbed: "Why art

thou cast down, O my soul? and why art thou disquieted within me?" (Psalm 42:11).

One preacher thought the motel business would be better than the ministry! *JEREMIAH* cried, "Oh that I had in the wilderness a lodging place of wayfaring men; that I might leave my people, and go from them," (Jeremiah 9:2).

Even a *prophet* lost confidence in people: *MICAH* cried, "The best of them is a brier: the most upright is sharper than a thorn hedge...Trust ye not in a friend" (Micah 7:4,5).

That *man of power, ELIJAH*, who outran horses for 30 miles, was fed miracle-meals by birds, called down fire on water-soaked sacrifices, once became so despondent he asked God to KILL him! (see 1 Kings 19).

JONAH, famous graduate of *"Whale University,"* had 120,000 converts in a single crusade. Yet later he begged God to take his life: "O Lord, take, I beseech Thee, my life from me; for it is better for me to die than to live" (Jonah 4:3).

As one of my longtime friends once stated: "Depression came when Jonah's personal *security* was more important than the *souls* of people."

Even the rich and wise SOLOMON confessed that he came to a place that he *"hated life"* (Ecclesiastes 2:17).

2.   Recognize The Danger Of Depression. A nonchalant mother shocked me: "Oh, my teenager stays depressed. I guess it's the stage he's in."

We treat depression too lightly. Depression can *result* in broken homes, physical breakdown, suicides and attempts, spiritual breakdown and countless other sorrows.

▶ *BROKEN HOMES*

A depressed mate exaggerates the negative side of his marriage, thinking, "Maybe I made a mistake." The parade of home-wrecking thoughts can become endless.

▶ *PHYSICAL BREAKDOWNS*

The National Institute of Mental Health has estimated that 125,000 Americans are hospitalized annually with depression. Another 200,000 get aid from psychiatrists.

▶ *SUICIDE*

Between 50,000 to 70,000 people commit suicide every year. It's estimated that over one million *attempt* it!

Two brokenhearted parents wrote me: "Our daughter attended church regularly. She appeared to be as happy as any normal 18 year old. Suddenly for a few days she became withdrawn. Last week we walked into her room and found her dead. *She took her own life.*"

Among all the persons being treated for depression in hospitals and clinics, nearly twenty percent are under 18. *The suicide rate among 15 to 19 year olds has DOUBLED in the last ten years.* In a national survey of persons between 18 to 74 years of age, those under 29 showed the highest incidence of depression.

By the way, *listening* parents often mean the difference between life and death for their frustrated teenagers.

▶ *SPIRITUAL BREAKDOWN*

Millions of Christians who wouldn't lie, cheat or kill are *immobilized* by frustrations and *paralyzed* in their pursuit of spiritual goals.

3.   Find The Basic Cause And Scriptural Solution To Your Depressions.

Though medical doctors speak of physical cycles and "highs and lows," *all depression is not necessarily physical.*

Be honest with yourself. Pinpoint your CAUSE of stress and take it to God.

Unconfessed sin is like a rock in your shoe. *Get it out!* If hidden sin is bringing inner frustration, no vacation or doctor will heal it.

"But your *iniquities* have separated between you and your God, and your sins have hid His face from you," (Isaiah 59:2).

Greed for gain will begin an avalanche of despondency. King Ahab's obsession for Naboth's vineyard affected the entire family: "He that is greedy of gain troubleth his own house;" (Proverbs 15:27). Jesus knew the danger: "Beware of covetousness: for a man's life consisteth not in the abundance of the things which he possesseth" (Luke 12:15).

Making comparisons is a sure road to frustration. One young pastor lamented, "When I hear a conference speaker share a personal success story, I feel like a *lawn mower* in a Cadillac showroom. Where is God when *I* pray?"

As one of my friends has said many times, "*Comparing* has brought more people unhappiness than they could ever imagine."

Taking criticism personally can bring depression to the person who forgets that, "Poverty and shame shall be to him that refuseth instruction:

but he that regardeth reproof shall be honoured" (Proverbs 13:18).

Many years ago while lunching with a pastor during a crusade in Dallas, Texas, he shared with me a wise observation: "Mike, our brethren help to keep us *balanced.*" I believe that. On the other hand, seeking *people approval* is a quick road to inner turmoil.

Fault-finding. One friend noted an inner depression when he indulged in revealing the flaws of others: "The words of a talebearer are as wounds," (Proverbs 18:8). God brought healing through the Word: "Whoso keepeth his mouth and his tongue keepeth his soul from troubles" (Proverbs 21:23). Guard your conversations. *Your words can create death or life.*

Impatience has impoverished thousands. Despondent youth, blinded to the benefits of *waiting,* become runaways, dropouts, premature parents and candidates for divorce.

An unforgiving attitude will drain your joy. David Wilkerson, author of "The Cross and the Switchblade," once said that a major problem he encountered among teens involved *bitterness and hatred toward parents.*

Many youth have found a *new world* of power and victorious living when a *forgiving spirit* was allowed to control their lives: "And when ye stand praying, *forgive,* if ye have ought against any: that your Father also which is in heaven may forgive you your trespasses" (Mark 11:25).

Fatigue is a major cause of depression. One renowned U.S. President refused to make major decisions at the end of the day. He insisted on a *rested* body and mind before committing himself on any issue.

Leaders have learned the power and strength of systematic recuperation.

WISDOM PRINCIPLE 45

When FATIGUE Walks In, FAITH Walks Out.

"For 10 years I lived knowing I missed God's perfect plan," one pastor confessed. "Weariness and mental fatigue blinded me to the fruits of my labors in a pastorate. Impulsively, I resigned. A few weeks later I realized the serious mistake. *Complete rest and relaxation with my family would have changed everything."*

If we refuse Christ's invitation to come apart and rest a while, we usually *come apart!*

4.   Take Immediate Action! In one of my crusades, one lady said that she had felt a cloud over her home for months. "Divorce," she had decided, "is the only answer." Unaware of her situation, I preached the message, *"Stay on Board."* "If you think the *'Sea of Divorce'* is better than your *'Ship of Marriage,'* you're in for the heartache of your life." That sentence lodged in her mind. And the next one was revolutionary for her. *"Stay on board* and give God a chance to bring you to a harbor!"

Putting her doubts aside, she placed new faith in God and vowed new efforts to make her marriage work. *One week later her husband was wonderfully converted to Christ.*

You should *anticipate* and *plan* for personal victory! Sometimes what begins in tragedy ends in *triumph!*

Consider Daniel—from lions' bait to honor.

The three Hebrew children—from fiery furnace to awe and approval.

Joseph—from a slave to a prime minister.

Jesus—from the Cross to the resurrection.

You can begin stepping out of depression now!

Enter into *joy.*

Enter into *rest.*

Enter into the *power-life.*

Enjoy the Winner's World!

You are more than a conqueror. *You can!* Paul said, *"I can do ALL things through Christ which strengtheneth me"* (Philippians 4:13). God has assured us, *"...My grace is sufficient for thee:"* (2 Corinthians 12:9).

Believe it! Do not let the words, the failures, the opinions of people crush you. Declare the promises of God. *Boldly. Aloud. Often.*

5.   Practice Three Secrets Of Power-Living Daily.

▶ *Respect the opinions of God concerning your life* (Scripture intake).

▶ *Habitualize your morning talks with God* (your commitment to one hour of prayer each day).

▶ *Faith-talk* (repeating *aloud* the viewpoint of God).

First: Your Wisdom Hour.

Someone has said, "Many people can find the secret of a *defeated* life in a *neglected Bible.*" Of all activities, satan will attack this practice vehemently.

Just make up your mind to read the Word daily! Start by starting. Do by *doing*.

Second: Your Morning Talks With God.

Oswald J. Smith has said the happiest moments of his life were during prayer and Bible time called his "Morning Watch." His praying *aloud* prevented wandering thoughts. His *walking* insured against dozing!

In Calcutta, India, a renowned missionary friend of mine often stopped in the midst of our conversations to pray for various needs. This is the secret behind God's great work in Calcutta.

He who majors on *achievements* will find his thrills short-lived; but the child of God who majors on his *relationship* to the Father will find the well of joy endless...springing up with new victories daily.

Third: Faith-Talk And Word Declaration.

It simply means to *say aloud* what is *written* in the *Word!* Your conversations will develop *problem-consciousness* or create *promise-awareness. Cultivate promise-awareness!*

As I write these words, I am looking across famous Lake Victoria in Kisumu, Kenya, East Africa. Sitting here in the home of outstanding missionaries, it is easy to forget that they must encounter cultural barriers, endure separation from children in boarding school, work alone without closest friends and confidants, prepare meals without the all-accommodating American supermarkets, and live with unbelievable delays and frustrating mechanical breakdowns.

Their Secret?

They refuse the *oral confession* of defeat. They have learned to *activate Word power by verbalizing praise.* With infectious laughter and humor, they practice Proverbs 16:24: *"Pleasant words are...health to the bones."* This turns miserable experiences into *praise sessions!* Small wonder their lives have counted so beautifully for God here in East Africa!

So remember, you are the property of God! You will not lose to depression. *You will win over every circumstance as long as He is your source and focus.*

☞ 18 ☜

LONELINESS, LOVE AND THE CHRISTIAN SINGLE

I read somewhere that there are more than 55 million single adults living in the U.S.A. today.

Many have experienced marriage and have lost their partner through divorce or death. For both, the transition to single life is often traumatic. Readjustment of schedules, loss of friendships, sudden aloneness can trigger an unbelievable crisis. It is an inside battle that requires time, and often painful, *spiritual* "surgery."

An interesting statement comes from a famous "single." The missionary, Apostle Paul, said: *"Art thou loosed from a wife? seek not a wife"* (1 Corinthians 7:27). At first glance, it seems to contradict Genesis 2:18 which says, *"It is not good that the man should be alone."*

Paul is simply saying, *"Concentrate on the present advantages."* Unpack and live where you are! Stop reliving yesterday. Memories are photographs of experiences. What we concentrate on, we *feel*. What we feel, we begin to perform. And our performance determines our sense of worth and self-esteem. It is satan's weapon to destroy the productivity of the present by forcing our concentration on the *past*.

Get involved with *present* opportunities. Develop your mind. Discipline your body. Open your heart to those around you.

My compassion for singles runs deep. I have experienced their emotional cycles, the sense of loss, the overwhelming loneliness. But I also know that during the pressure zone, God becomes very real. That pressure zone is also a *growth* zone.

Emotional Cycles

Singles usually experience constantly changing emotional cycles. Sometimes we sit in our apartment or home thinking, "God, when are You going to send *somebody* I can share my dreams and plans with? *Please,* God!" Then the very next day, "Whew! I'm glad nobody's here to hassle me!"

It is part of maturing. What we *think* we need and what we actually need are often two different things.

Greatness Is A Process

► Your experience with *emptiness*...prepares you for the *filling*.

► Your experience of *loneliness*...develops appreciation for *companionship*.

► The experience of *doubt*...forces us to dig for what we *really* believe.

► The testing of *sincerity* in others...develops *your discerning* abilities.

► *Timing* is the Golden Word in the World of Wisdom. It will be the key to the treasures you dream of unlocking. There is a time to be *aggressive*. There is a time to be *gentle*.

"To every thing there is a season, and a time to every purpose under the heaven:" (Ecclesiastes 3:1).

"The Lord is good unto them that wait for Him" (Lamentations 3:25).

Winning Secrets For Singles

The most powerful force in the world is love. It breaks through the barricades of prejudice, tradition and selfishness. It is the basis for motivation: The labors of a father, the toils of a mother are rooted in that invisible ingredient called love.

To Love Someone Is To Place High Value On Them. "Falling in love" is the mental picture that illustrates *dethronement* of self and the *elevation* of another.

An important question every *single* should ask is, "Why am I really attracted to this person? Is it simply good looks? Talents? Mutual interests?"

Many times we actually love a characteristic or *quality* in someone *rather than the person.* Memories of past harsh treatment will accentuate and magnify the gentleness of a new friend. Financial pressures will exaggerate the attractiveness of financial security.

Many singles have accepted *less* than God's very best simply because of loneliness.

Loneliness Can Cloud Your Judgment

Be honest with yourself. *Discern the dominate basis of attraction.* Name it. If the person in your life now is a spiritual strength or simply helps you to "climb socially," *name it for what it is.* If it is simply feeding physical desires, to deceive yourself will be *costly.*

Stay strong. *Don't let temporary loneliness create a permanent problem.* And remember, "Blessed is the man that endureth temptation: for when he is tried, he shall receive the crown of life, which the Lord hath promised to them that love Him" (James 1:12).

A Word Of Caution For Overgivers!

Do not give to others in proportion to your total capacity or ability to give. *Discern the size of their cup, and give according to their capacity to receive.* A gallon poured in a pint container is not only *waste,* but drowns those who receive, and *weakens the ability of the giver to "sow" again.*

Factors In Discerning True Love

How do we discern *true* love? How do we know when we are "in love?" How can we have the assurance that someone truly loves *us?*

Many argue over this thing of "falling in love," but let's avoid quibbling and admit: God has to give you *a very special desire* and love for that person who excites your desire for *commitment.*

3 Proofs Of Uncommon Love

1.   **Uncommon Love Does Not Fear.** Fear is distrust and lack of confidence. "There is no fear in love; but perfect love casteth out fear: because fear hath torment. He that feareth is not made perfect in love" (1 John 4:18). Something is missing when fear is present. It may be evidence of the wrong

person or the wrong timing. Be cautious.

2.   Uncommon Love Wants To Give. Love wants to contribute to another's needs: "For God so loved the world that He *gave* His only begotten Son, that whosoever believeth in Him should not perish, but have everlasting life" (John 3:16). True love results in the investment of time, effort and even finances in another. Ministering to someone you love should become a joy.

3.   Uncommon Love Anticipates The Needs Of Others. Jesus proved this with Zacchaeus, and with the Samaritan woman at the well: "...for your heavenly Father knoweth that ye have need of all these things. But seek ye first the kingdom of God, and His righteousness; and all these things shall be added unto you" (Matthew 6:32,33).

As you sow your love into those around you expect God to bless you beyond your greatest expectations.

"What You Make Happen For Others, God Will Make Happen For You" (see Ephesians 6:8).

The Proof Of Love
Is The
Investment Of Time.

-MIKE MURDOCK

~ 19 ~

YOUTH AND THE SEX TRAP

"She is the finest girl in our church," said the pastor to me with pride. "Her consecration and Christian testimony are both tremendous. I just wish all our youth were like her."

So after my sermon on the closing night of the crusade, I was a bit surprised when the teenager asked for a few minutes of counseling about a personal problem. Within moments she was sobbing. "Please help me. I'm so confused I'm about to lose my mind. My parents, my pastor and church friends think I am a fantastic Christian. But the truth is, I live a double life. I am so messed up morally with some boys at school that I'm miserable and want to die."

With tears streaming down her face she told me her sad, sordid, but familiar story. Then came her question: "If I love God and the Bible—and I do —*then why do I fight such tremendous problems with sex?* I feel trapped. I don't know how to escape. Is there any hope for me?"

Of course, this young woman is far from the only one in this condition. Thousands of people who sincerely want to live right and pleasing to God are fighting this same battle. They, too, have fallen into what I call the "Sex Trap." They are caught up in an unending struggle between sexual excitement and sensual pleasure on the one hand and the grip of guilt, remorse and fear on the other. *They feel trapped between their desire for moral and spiritual purity and the physical appetites of the body.*

There Is A Way Out

As powerful and inescapable as the Sex Trap seems to be, there is a way out for you. *You have the power to be free.* The following pages can completely change your outlook on life. I want to share some encouragement and insights to help you.

This chapter is not for the rebel who is determined to have his own way, no matter the consequences. It is not for the know-it-all, the arrogant, the hypocrite or the weakling looking for justification for his failure. These pages are for the sincere person aware of the opposing pulls within—the pull toward God and truth and the opposing pull toward immoral thoughts and actions. This chapter is for YOU if you want help and are willing to accept it.

The key to getting out of the Sex Trap is understanding. You must come to a clear *understanding* of yourself and how you are made. You must understand the *drives* and *desires* God put within you and *why* He put them there. And you must be aware that the enemy tries to turn these normal, healthy drives into something dirty and destructive.

In Proverbs 7, the wise man, Solomon, writes a graphic description of the Sex Trap in operation. I urge you to take a few moments to read it. This passage is about a girl and a boy and their physical desires for sexual gratification. It is a story of seduction, sin and shame. In this case, a prostitute lures a young man to her bedroom for a night of pleasure. But Solomon tells us the boy walked into a trap. For "Her house is the way to hell, going down to the chambers of death" (Proverbs 7:27).

Let us seek to understand some key words that will lead to freedom and release from the Sex Trap.

Desire

There is an attraction—a *pull* between men and women. Call it chemistry—sex appeal—physical and emotional attraction—or whatever you want. But it is there. *And it was put there by God.*

It started in the Garden of Eden. Why do you suppose God placed Adam and Eve there instead of Adam and *Edward?* Because God knew it was good for a man and a woman to dwell together. And He placed within them a basic instinct to desire and enjoy the company of the opposite sex. It is a desire to share...to *give.* God placed it there for a divine purpose—to benefit not only one man and one woman, but the entire human race.

Some people seem to have the mistaken belief that this desire in and of itself is evil—that it comes from satan. They say if a person is really a Christian he "won't be bothered" by sexual desire. If a person prays, reads the Bible and goes to church, the opposite sex just won't appeal to him, they say. Don't you believe it. *Desire is normal.* And it is not evil until it becomes twisted into a lustful *obsession* for sheer *physical self-gratification.*

Direction

The key to whether desire is good or bad is the direction it takes. Desire can be the motivating force that causes two young people to grow and mature. It is a drive that ultimately leads them to leave their parents and form a new household, "And they twain shall be one flesh:" (Mark 10:8).

Channeled in the *right* direction, desire leads to a happy, Christian home that will obey God's command to multiply and replenish the earth. This direction is pleasing to God and results in a man-woman relationship that is healthy, filled with love and mutual respect.

WISDOM PRINCIPLE 46

Loneliness Is Not A Loss Of Affection, But The Loss Of Direction.

Tragically, your desires can also take the opposite direction. It can cause you to *withdraw* from God and the way of righteousness. Some people let their desire steer them *into areas of temptation* that sooner or later overpower them.

In the Bible, Samson ran *toward* the wrong woman. Joseph, tempted by Potiphar's wife, ran from her. One enjoyed the company of immorality—the other delighted in God. One was a loser...the other a winner. And it was all a matter of *direction*.

Deception

In almost every case of sexual sin, there is deception involved. It can take many forms: "If you really love me, you'll prove it. Everybody else is doing it. It's all right because we love each other. No one will get hurt. Just this one time, then never again."

> **WISDOM PRINCIPLE 47**
>
> ➤━◆━◄
>
> *Immaturity Is The Inability To Delay Self-Gratification.*

Sexual deception presents only *one* side of the picture. Like all traps, it is made to entice—not repel. What is the bait in the Sex Trap? "It will be so exciting and satisfying. It will give us so much pleasure. It will make us happy." *Anything forbidden usually excites.*

But like all traps, *when the bait is stripped away*, there are strong, powerful jaws lined with sharp, cutting teeth ready to crush you and tear your life to shreds. Instead of the pleasure it promises, the Sex Trap delivers *pain* and *heartbreak*.

Satan uses deception to make people believe they can sin and not pay the consequences—that they can steal the honey and not get stung. Only after they have gone beyond the point of no return—past the bright lights, attractive setting and flattering words—do they find they have been deceived. Then they are *trapped* by the agonizing reality of the lonely heart, *the tortured conscience*, the tattered, ragged remnants of self-respect.

In every deception, there is the *deceiver* and the *deceived*. There is the one who will say or do whatever is necessary to get his own way. And there is the one who ends up with the heartache, the guilt, the pain. There is the hunter...and the hunted. There is the "fooler"....and the fool.

In Solomon's story (Proverbs 7), the woman was the deceiver. But often it is a man who deceives a woman. The woman in the proverb *flattered* the young man with *words*. She made herself—her body —*the bait* in the Sex Trap, putting on appealing and alluring clothing. Never mind that her actions were disloyal to her own friends and family, she thought *only of her own desire*. She was *lonely*... restless. She wanted an immediate response—a *physical* gratification. And she was interested only in temporary pleasure—she wanted the young man only *until the morning* (verse 18). She was the deceiver, and she kept talking until she got her way: "With her much fair speech she caused him to yield, with the flattering of her lips she forced him" (verse 21).

An Ox, Fool And Bird

And what about the deceived? *Someone has to be the loser,* and Solomon describes them in pretty graphic terms. He says the person who allows himself to be deceived is headed for destruction, "...as an ox goeth to the slaughter, or as a fool to the correction of the stocks...as a bird hasteth the snare, and knoweth not that it is for his life" (verses 22-23).

An ox. A fool. A bird. Not a very flattering picture, is it? But, is it you? Are you walking blindly and without resistance toward your own destruction?

Oh, I know how clever the deceivers are. I know how skillfully the deception is presented. The magazines, the music, the screen, the seductive voices all make it seem so much fun, so romantic, so beautiful, so pleasant and satisfying. *But can you look beyond the big lie and see what is on the other side?* What happens *after* the night of passion passes and *you are left alone* to face yourself in the mirror in the cold clear light of day? How will you make yourself "feel good" then?

WISDOM PRINCIPLE 48

Your Self-Worth Is Not Determined By Your Past Mistakes, But By Your Willingness To Recognize Them.

Go talk to those who have been deceived. Talk to the boy or girl who couldn't wait to go "all the way." Ask the husband who got restless how he feels *now?* Talk to the wife who felt unloved and see if she found fulfillment. Go see the unwed mother who has faced the rejection of society and who feels her mistake will last forever. Try comforting the illegitimate child who feels that no one wants him. Go see what it is like to be the deceived...the victim.

Is that what you want?

Attention Or Admiration?

Oh, my dear teenage friend, please listen to this message from the depths of my heart: there is a vast difference between getting attention and receiving admiration. Take great care that you are not deceived into mistaking one for the other.

How do you recognize a deceiver? Test the *attitudes* of each person you consider for a date. Can you detect a rebellious spirit or arrogance toward *God?* Is there disrespect for *parents?* Does he or she have a "line" that is mostly double talk? Is that person interested only in fun and good times and never serious about anything? Do you sense a lazy, unforgiving or lustful spirit? Is there an *inner warning* inside you that something is wrong about the person, even though there may be a simultaneous attraction. These are your *warning signs.*

Decision

Sometime...somewhere...*you have to make a decision.* You must choose either to win or lose the battle to avoid falling into the Sex Trap. At some point you will pass beyond the protective influence of your parents, your pastor, your church. Sooner or later the full responsibility for your actions rests squarely upon your shoulders. *In the courtroom of your own conscience* you will have to weigh your moral and spiritual values against the persuasive arguments of the deceiver. The choice will be yours:

► the *flesh*...or the spiritual
► the *physical*...instead of the heart cry
► the *now*...instead of tomorrow
► the *temporary*...instead of the eternal plan
► crowd *approval*...or God's respect
► a moment's *pleasure*...or God's Master Plan?

If you choose to be deceived, then nothing or no one can stop you.

If you choose what you know in your heart is right and pleasing to God, it will lead you away from the snaring pitfall of the Sex Trap. Yes, the decision could cost you a boyfriend or girlfriend... *if* he or she is a deceiver. *But not for long.* When young people are willing to give up companions who are bad for them, I believe they will soon find the person who will be the joy of their life. *God is a perfect matchmaker!*

Destruction Or Deliverance

The person who chooses habitual, consistent wrong will be burdened with...disappointment... disgrace...destruction.

How disappointing to find that what you thought was so great and so much fun lasts *only for moments.* But the *ache* in your heart *keeps pounding away* when your "friend" has left, the lights are turned out, and you are—alone. What a let-down to find that people can only meet the temporary, surface needs for affection and companionship. But what are you to do when you must turn within and face the God of eternity *by yourself?*

What shame and humiliation you feel when you must go out to face the world again after falling into the Sex Trap. Disgrace? One girl said, "I felt dirty— like everybody who looked at me could tell."

A boy said, "I didn't want to look anybody straight in the eyes."

And somehow, it seems, someone always does find out—and the news spreads like wildfire. Strange thing, but where are all those liberated, modern-thinking people you were told were everywhere? Why are so many staying away from you...looking down on you? Where is the loyalty and respect you always enjoyed from your friends? *Where are your friends?*

Destruction—yes, if that is what you choose,

that is what you will get. You will destroy your own *sensitivity to God* and to your *conscience*. You destroy your own self-respect, a quality that is absolutely essential to your well-being, and one that is tremendously difficult to regain once it is lost.

And now we come to the girl I told you about in the beginning. Everyone at home and at the church still thought she was a super person. But she realized she had fallen into the Sex Trap. The word was out at school. She had suffered the disappoint-ment...even some of the disgrace. And she sensed she was on the downward slide to destruction.

"I know I'm doing wrong. But I can't help it. The temptation is too great. I can't resist—it's stronger than I am. I can't say no. I know what's right, but I keep doing wrong. Is there any hope for me? Or is it too late? Can I be delivered?"

WISDOM PRINCIPLE 49

Repentance Is Always The First Step To Recovery.

Let me share with you the same answer I gave her. And it will help you, just as it helped her find deliverance and freedom from the Sex Trap.

There is a way out. There is an answer. Jesus said, "I am the way," (John 14:6). And that is your only hope of deliverance—through the forgiveness and deliverance of the Savior, Jesus Christ.

You say, "But Mike, I'm in so deep, I'm really messed up."

The Bible says Jesus has already taken care of your situation. How? He "...gave Himself for our sins, that He might deliver us from this present evil world," (Galatians 1:4).

"But you don't know all the bad things I've done. It's worse than you think. I'll never be good for anything again."

WISDOM PRINCIPLE 50

Failure Will Last Only As Long As You Permit It.

That's not the way God sees you. He has reserved a place just for you in His kingdom. How do I know that? Read it for yourself in 2 Timothy 4:18: "And the Lord shall deliver me from every evil work, and will preserve me unto His heavenly kingdom:"

"OK, I'm convinced. What do I have to do to be forgiven?"

Again, the answer is right there in your Bible: "If we confess our sins, He is faithful and just to forgive us our sins, and to cleanse us from all unrighteousness" (1 John 1:9).

Who do you confess to? To God, because He is the only One Who can deliver you.

Regardless of how many times you have gotten free and have fallen again, *there is deliverance for you.* Start "practicing" the presence of God. What do I mean by that? Simply this—*realize* that God is with you all the time. *Depend on His presence to uphold you and keep you strong.* Do not go anywhere and allow yourself to get in any situation where you are not comfortable in His presence. If it means changing friends—change them. If it means changing your *habits* and *environment*—do it. Don't be afraid of what people will think, or say, or do. Be bold in this assurance: "Be not afraid of their faces: for I am with thee to deliver thee, saith the Lord" (Jeremiah 1:8).

It is that simple—really, it is. If you have been honest and sincere before God, He has forgiven you and washed you white as snow, though your sins were as scarlet. Now you have become a new creature— you are *born again*. I want to help you pray:

"Thank You, Lord for forgiving my sins, for lifting my guilt, for giving me new purity. Help me never to be caught again in the Sex Trap. I am weak, but You are strong. Give me as much of Your strength as I need. There have been wrong desires in my life. Take them away, O Lord, along with every tendency to lie or deceive. Be Lord of my life. I present my body as a temple of Your Spirit—fill me and keep me I pray in Jesus' name, Amen."

Discovery

To discover a new truth is a marvelous feeling. To discover the truth about *God and His power to deliver* is really a thrill. It is the greatest discovery of your life.

By now you have made some important discoveries about the Sex Trap. You may have found that:

> ▶ Sin looks good, but feels *bad* in the heart.
> ▶ Sowing maybe fun, but the *reaping* is devastation.
> ▶ The physical may be satisfying temporarily, but the *heart* still cries.
> ▶ What you thought would bring happiness

brought *misery* instead.

You have also discovered that there is deliverance from the Sex Trap through the *power of God*. You have discovered that God's forgiveness brings real, genuine peace into your life. *You will never be the same again.*

Now, I want you to discover still more truths that will help you remain strong and free. They are part of God's plan for you. These new discoveries will help you change your *thought-life*...perhaps even your lifestyle. And when that happens, you will discover the *good life is possible right now*. That powerful discovery comes through discipline.

Discipline

The key to victory, power and reward in every part of your life is *personal discipline*. Every athletic champion and Olympic winner practices discipline. In fact, almost without exception, winners are successful because of discipline, which gives birth to *success-habits*.

Not only does discipline hone the mind and condition the body, it produces an important side effect—*security*. Just as a child, who receives discipline from its parents, feels secure in their love, so the person who practices self-discipline is confident that good things will happen to them instead of bad. Paul said, "...I keep under my body, and bring it into subjection:" (1 Corinthians 9:27).

So the athlete knows what his body will do when he calls on it to perform in the contest. The scholar knows his mind will produce the answers he needs because he has *disciplined* it to be alert and prepared.

And the Christian young person knows how he will react in the face of temptation because he has *disciplined* his moral and spiritual nature to *overcome* evil.

6 Areas Of Your Life That Must Be Disciplined

1.   **Discipline Your Conversation.** Speak always in positive terms, from a position of faith and awareness of what God wants from you. Avoid negative words, such as "I can't...I'm weak...I always fail." Instead, say, "I can overcome all sin. I am getting stronger in the Lord. I can do all things through Christ, which strengtheneth me."

> **WISDOM PRINCIPLE 51**
>
> *Men Do Not Really Decide Their Future... They Decide Their Habits — Then, Their Habits Decide Their Future.*

2.   **Discipline Your Reading Habits.** Be sure you spend at least ten minutes each morning in the Word of God. There is no possibility of living the true victorious, happy life apart from a daily intake of the Scriptures. They will make you strong and keep you free: "The law of his God is in his heart; none of his steps shall slide" (Psalm 37:31). Be sure everything else you read contributes to your well-being.

3.   **Discipline Your Prayer Life.** Stay in constant, personal contact with God. Be sure you are on speaking terms with Him. Develop and cultivate an up-to-date prayer list.

4.   Discipline Your Friendships. Refuse to associate with losers who pull you down. Choose friends who will be the kind of associates you'd like to spend your whole life with.

5.   Discipline Yourself With Regard To The Music You Listen To, The Television Programs You Watch And The Entertainment You Choose. Control the circumstances that are within your power. One teenage girl finally admitted to me that she had schemed to find ways to be alone with her boyfriend when she knew she was too weak to say no to wrong. If you can't refuse temptation— at least you can *avoid* it. But it takes discipline.

6.   Finally, Discipline Yourself In Church Attendance. Develop inner strength by exposing yourself often to the atmosphere of a spiritual church service. Honor the spiritual mentors God places in your life.

There you have it—*a formula for success that will work for you*. It is a way to overcome and be free of the tragic snare of the Sex Trap. God wants you to be *free*. And I want you to be free, too.

All Men Fall.
The Great Ones
Simply Get Back Up.

-MIKE MURDOCK

∼ 20 ∼

HOW TO TURN YOUR MISTAKES INTO MIRACLES

This is a *human* world. You will find that mistakes are just a part of your daily life. Mistakes happen on the job, in your choice of friends, and even in financial decisions.

WISDOM PRINCIPLE 52

Yesterday's Failure...CAN Become The Catalyst For Tomorrow's Success.

Though some mistakes can be devastating, the majority of your mistakes can be turned around for your good!

Yesterday's failure can become *today's* success. *Tragedies* can become *triumphs.*

You can change the direction of your life! *You* can step *out* of failure and into a victorious and successful life. God, your Creator and Heavenly Father has anticipated your problem areas and has laid out a *plan* for turning your mistakes into miracles!!

Proverbs 24:16: "For a just man falleth seven times, and riseth up again:"

Psalm 37:23,24: "The steps of a good man are ordered by the Lord: and He delighteth in his way.

Though he fall, he shall not be utterly cast down: for the Lord upholdeth him with His hand."

15 Power Keys That Can Turn Your Mistakes Into Miracles

1. Accept Your Humanity.

You are not God. Neither do you have "angel wings!" The possibilities of your making a mistake are one hundred percent. The *nature* of your mistakes and *what you do about them* determine your success. God anticipated your weaknesses. "Like as a father pitieth his children, so the Lord pitieth them that fear Him. For He knoweth our frame; He remembereth that we are dust" (Psalm 103:13,14).

True, some use the flimsy comment, "I'm just human," as a "cop-out" and cover-up instead of a motivation for higher principles. Thousands who learn to *accept* themselves as human beings learn to enjoy life so much better.

2. Admit Your Mistake.

Recognize and confess it to *yourself.* Do not justify it. Do not lie to yourself. The Scriptures say: "He that covereth his sins shall not prosper: but whoso confesseth and forsaketh them shall have mercy" (Proverbs 28:13). Confess your mistake to *God*.

"If we confess our sins, He is faithful and just to forgive us our sins, and to cleanse us from all unrighteousness" (1 John 1:9).

Confess your mistake to *others* who were damaged by your mistake.

"And when ye stand praying, forgive, if ye have ought against any: that your Father also which is in heaven may forgive you your trespasses" (Mark 11:25).

Caution: there are exceptions. When your confession would do more to *destroy* faith and confidence in the mind of another, confess to God *alone*. "In the multitude of words there wanteth not sin: but he that refraineth his lips is wise" (Proverbs 10:19).

> **WISDOM PRINCIPLE 53**
>
> ⇒≻●≺⇐
>
> *If God Cushioned Every Blow, You Would Never Learn To Grow.*

3. Assign The Responsibility Of The Mistake To Those Truly Responsible.

If others are involved, you must allow them to accept their own share of the blame. Assuming all responsibility for others opens the door to bitterness, resentment and self-pity. Besides, you add to their own success by forcing them to account for themselves. Parents who always "cover" for little Johnny or Susie destroy their children's chances for maturity. "Chasten thy son while there is hope, and let not thy soul spare for his crying" (Proverbs 19:18).

"I've got to go get my husband out of the bar tonight, he's drinking again," a heartbroken lovely lady told me one night.

I replied, "Why?"

She looked surprised. "Well...uh...he...uh."

I said, "If you keep cushioning the fall, he'll never quit jumping. *You've got to let him hit the bottom.* Then, and only then will he want to reach for the top."

**4. Review The Other Possible
Alternatives Available To You At The Time Of
Your Mistake.**

Obviously, you made a wrong move. What were
the *options* at the time? Could you have done it
differently? Did you do your very best? "For which
of you, intending to build a tower, sitteth not down
first, and counteth the cost, whether he have
sufficient to finish it?" (Luke 14:28).

Sometimes what *appears* to be a mistake was
the *only* possible decision at the time! Don't waste
valuable time on unavoidable past circumstances.
Perhaps a mistake wasn't made at all!

On the other hand, by carefully evaluating the
past, you will avoid making the same mistake again.

**5. Name The People Or Circumstances
That Were Influencing You When You Made
Your Mistake.**

A minister friend once told me, "Mike, I missed
God's perfect will during ten long years of my life."

"What caused it?" I asked.

"I got overtired," he said. "I overreacted to
criticism from a disgruntled deacon. I just up and
resigned my church before God was finished with
my ministry there. It was the biggest mistake of my
entire life."

Fatigue warped his judgment

Are you watching too much television?
Neglecting consistent church attendance? Involved
in unhealthy friendships? Is it your ego? Be honest!

Your dreams and goals can be destroyed by
listening to the wrong advice. Even *sickness* can

greatly affect your decision-making. A frustrated friend may be creating a climate of discontent for you. "He that walketh with wise men shall be wise: but a companion of fools shall be destroyed" (Proverbs 13:20).

6. **Be Willing To Taste The Pain Of Your Mistake.**

There are times God wants us to *feel* the *hurt* of our wrongs. In Luke 15, the prodigal son *"came to himself"* when he became so hungry. "He would fain have filled his belly with the husks that the swine did eat" (verse 16).

Pain can motivate you. God may allow you to crash! *If He cushioned every blow, you would never grow.*

WISDOM PRINCIPLE 54

Confession Is A Faith-Releaser Into Total Restoration.

However, I assure you, your Heavenly Father will not allow your suffering and ache to be a permanent feeling. He will use it to develop a *humility,* a *compassion* for others and a *reminder* of why Jesus Christ died on Calvary for the sins of the world: "But He knoweth the way that I take: when He hath tried me, I shall come forth as gold" (Job 23:10).

The Psalmist said: "It is good for me that I have been afflicted; that I might learn Thy statutes" (Psalm 119:71).

Hebrews 5:8 says: "Though He were a Son, yet learned He obedience by the things which He suffered."

7. **Write A List Of The Personal Lessons**

You Have Learned And Any Current Alternatives.

Take a sheet of paper and "Write the vision and make it plain" (Habakkuk 2:2). Ask yourself these questions.

"What *weaknesses in myself* does this mistake reveal?"

"What have I learned about *others* during this time?"

"What do the *Scriptures* teach in regard to my mistake?"

Take time to *think*...to *hear* with your *heart* what you can understand through this time of learning. Read and study the lives of people who made the same mistake and how they recovered. Focus on what you can do *now,* and begin taking the necessary steps toward recovery.

8. Stop Talking To Everyone About Your Mistake.

A few choice friends will gladly lend an ear as you release your pent-up hurt. You may need it...with the *right* people. However, it is even more effective to discuss it with God. "In the day when I cried Thou answeredst me, and strengthenedst me with strength in my soul" (Psalm 138:3). "I sought the Lord, and He heard me, and delivered me from all my fears" (Psalm 34:4).

You see, too many times we display our weaknesses *unnecessarily.* It magnifies our mistakes and puts ammunition in the hands of our enemies. Stop putting yourself down! Make up your mind you are *not* losing, you are *learning!*

"He that hath knowledge spareth his words:"

(Proverbs 17:27). "Give instruction to a wise man, and he will be yet wiser: teach a just man, and he will increase in learning" (Proverbs 9:9).

Be kind but firm in refusing others the liberty to focus on your past failures. "Brethren, I count not myself to have apprehended: but this one thing I do, forgetting those things which are behind...I press toward the mark for the prize of the high calling of God in Christ Jesus. Let us therefore, as many as be perfect, be thus minded: and if in any thing ye be otherwise minded, God shall reveal even this unto you" (Philippians 3:13-15).

I suggest you actually memorize Isaiah 43:18,19: "Remember ye not the former things, neither consider the things of old. Behold, I will do a new thing; now it shall spring forth; shall ye not know it? I will even make a way in the wilderness, and rivers in the desert."

9. Make Restitution With Those You Have Wronged Or Hurt.

True repentance involves restitution—mending broken fences. One definition of restitution is "the *final restoration* of all things and persons to harmony with God's will." Restitution is a *faith-releasing* principle that purifies your conscience. It unties the hands of God to work freely in your behalf. "If a man shall steal an ox, or a sheep, and kill it, or sell it; he shall restore five oxen for an

WISDOM PRINCIPLE 55

Your Contribution To Others Determines What God Will Contribute To You.

ox, and four sheep for a sheep" (Exodus 22:1). "And Zacchaeus stood, and said unto the Lord; Behold, Lord, the half of my goods I give to the poor; and if I have taken any thing from any man by false accusation, I restore him fourfold" (Luke 19:8).

Several years ago, a man was having marital problems, stomach pains and could not sleep at night. He broke down and confessed to me that he had embezzled money from his company.

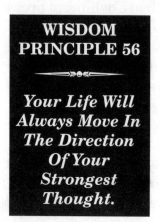

WISDOM PRINCIPLE 56

Your Life Will Always Move In The Direction Of Your Strongest Thought.

"You must make it right," I insisted. "Go to your president and totally level with him. Admit your mistake."

Though he feared losing his job, the man truly recognized the value of restitution. Guess what happened! *Not only was he permitted to keep his job, but later received a promotion from the president who respected his openness and new convictions!*

Pain is merely a passage to a miracle.

10. Allow A Season Of Time For Your Recovery.

It is natural to want an *"instant"* change in your circumstances. Take for instance, the emotional cycle following a divorce...loneliness...anger...guilt... bitterness...frustration...emptiness...depression... past memories. How do you cope with these? It is not always as easy as glib-tongued friends may try to make it appear.

It *simply* takes time *for total healing.*

Of course, there are things you can do to *hasten* the healing, just as it is possible to *slow* your healing process. The wisest man who ever lived said: "To every thing there is a season, and a time to every purpose" (Ecclesiastes 3:1).

But, do not weary of waiting for your complete miracle. Give yourself space: "And let us not be weary in well doing: for in due season we shall reap, if we faint not" (Galatians 6:9).

Meanwhile, during your "Recovery Zone," learn all you can, cultivate compassion, exercise faith, and develop control in all areas of your life.

11. Help Someone Else Receive Their Miracle.

Jesus Christ is our master example of concentrating on the success of *others*. He literally is a Success-Maker. He reprogrammed the mentality of losers.

Jesus Cared About Others

He took the time:

...to compliment (see Matthew 8:10).

...to heal the sick (see Matthew 8:16).

...to forgive sin (see Matthew 9:2).

...to advise ministers (see Matthew 10:1-42).

...to teach the unlearned (see Matthew 5,6,7).

...to expose frauds (see Matthew 23).

He created *success situations* for people.

Look around you! What can you do now to be a better employee on your job? A better husband or wife? A better friend? Proverbs 3:27 says: "Withhold not good from them to whom it is due, when it is in the power of thine hand to do it."

"Render therefore to all their dues: tribute to whom tribute is due; custom to whom custom; fear to whom fear; honour to whom honour" (Romans 13:7).

"Knowing that whatsoever good thing any man doeth, the same shall he receive of the Lord, whether he be bond or free" (Ephesians 6:8). Never forget the greatest Wisdom Principle in scriptural success: "What You Make Happen For Others, God Will Make Happen For You!"

12. Develop The Winner's Mentality.

You become what you think. So, start hanging "success photographs" on the walls of your own mind!

...Picture yourself in *health*.

...Picture yourself in *prosperity*.

...Picture yourself in a *happy marriage*.

...Picture yourself as an *overcomer*.

...Picture yourself as *victorious*.

When you control your thoughts, you control your life: "...Whatsoever things are true...honest... just...pure...lovely...of good report; if there be any virtue, if there be any praise, *think on these things*" (Philippians 4:8).

Visualize what you want to *materialize!*

Sometime ago I bought a car. With it, I received an owner's handbook on how to operate it, how to solve possible problems. It was to help me enjoy driving my new car, and avoid some frustrating situations.

God, the Creator, provided the same service to you and me to enjoy living in His world. That Success Handbook is called the Bible. It is your source for How To Live On Planet Earth. Without it, you may easily sabotage your life.

Read the Bible often. It will place positive and powerful mind-photographs in your thinking. You will begin to understand God, others and yourself in a beautiful new light!

13. Celebrate Even Your Smallest Accomplishments!

When you find a parking space exactly where you wanted...a dress you wanted on sale for half price...a gasoline station open when your tank shows empty—*talk about it!* Immediately verbalize a big, *"Thanks, Father!"* Tell your friends!

WISDOM PRINCIPLE 57

You Are Never As Far From A Miracle As It First Appears.

Learn to appreciate these "little" blessings! Cultivate the "attitude of gratitude!" Look for the good in others. Look for the good in yourself! Recognize your own accomplishments no matter how insignificant they may appear. Jesus told a great truth in Matthew 25 when the principle of recognition and rewards was given: "...thou has been faithful over a few things, I will make thee ruler over many things" (verses 21,23).

Express thanksgiving for the "little" blessings, and you will see those "bigger blessings" begin to follow.

14. Begin This Very Moment.

Start today. God put you and this book together. God is a *now* God. He wants you to become a *Winner* this very day. Right now pray this prayer aloud:

"Father, I need You. I want You. Forgive me of

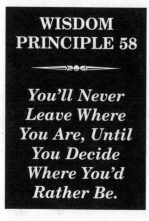

WISDOM PRINCIPLE 58

You'll Never Leave Where You Are, Until You Decide Where You'd Rather Be.

every mistake I have made with my life. I accept Jesus Christ as the Lord and Master of my life. I now receive Your forgiveness, and believe that You will begin to fill my heart and life with peace and joy from this very moment. Fill me with Your Holy Spirit as I enter the winner's world! I place all the memories of yesterday's mistake at the cross of Calvary. I thank You for sending the right people into my life this week to help me develop and grow into a powerful winner for You. In Jesus' name, Amen."

15.   Never, Never, Never Quit.

You've started. You have read this book this far through which shows *you have what it takes to be a winner! You can make it!*

You may experience a few setbacks, a few moments of doubt and confusion. This is normal and will not linger. Immediately, say aloud, "I am not a quitter, I am a winner! Nothing can stop me." Make this your confession: "I can do all things through Christ which strengtheneth me:" (Philippians 4:13). Remember 1 John 4:4: "...greater is He that is in you, than he that is in the world."

"The Lord upholdeth all that fall, and raiseth up all those that be bowed down" (Psalm 145:14).

≈ 21 ≈

If You Want A Miracle, Do These Things

Everybody wants a miracle.

Some will drive 500 miles to see one. Someone else will fly 3,000 miles to *experience* one for themselves.

Some do not even believe they exist. Others believe they only happen by *accident*.

WISDOM PRINCIPLE 59

The Picture That Stays In Your Mind Will Happen In Time.

The truth is...*miracles are not accidents.*

They are not the Master's manipulations of human "mannequins." Nor are they the performances of an egotistical, divine "show off."

Miracles happen to people who *need* them, *want* them, and *reach* for them.

7 Steps To Receive Your Miracles

1. Name Your Desired Miracle.

You cannot *find* until you *define.*

Jesus asked the blind man to explain what he wanted. Jesus was not ignorant. He simply needed a *commitment* to establish the contract (see Matthew 18:18-19)! *Many people do not like where they are, but they have never decided where they want to be.*

Often, I fly up to 20,000 miles per month. The airlines do not sell me tickets based on my point of departure, but rather on my desired *destination. I can't leave until I've decided where I want to land.* My treasured friend, Nancy Harmon, wrote it in her great song, *"Name It and Claim It."*

2.   Confirm Your Scriptural Grounds For Pursuing Your Desired Miracle.

Search the Word. *Stand* on the promise God inspires. *Avoid* any justification of failure. Do you want to really impress God? *Then believe* what He said. "God is not a man, that He should lie" (see Numbers 23:19).

3.   Ask For The Miracle.

"Ask, and it shall be given you...For every one that asketh receiveth;" (Matthew 7:7,8). Make a demand on the ability of God. Jesus said once that someone had touched Him...for a desired reason and purpose. Be persistent. *Reach* for your miracle.

4.   Don't Feed Your Friendships With Doubters.

Some "friends" may criticize you. They may even suggest that you lower your sights and "accept things as they are." Dare to resist. God made you to *climb,* not crawl! He made you to *fly,* not fall! *Feed your mind* on the Word. Surround yourself with tapes and books that fuel the fire of your faith within you.

5.   Talk Power-Talk Daily.

Stop talking defeat. Stop discussing your fears, doubts and unbelief. Talk your *expectations,* not your disappointing experiences. When others plant Seeds of fear, speak aloud and boldly what God *has spoken in His Word*. You were born to win. You were *born to taste the grapes of God's blessings!*

6.   Make An Effort.

Visualize yourself with the completed miracle.

Never underestimate the power and influence of your God given mind-machine. It is a "camera." The photo file it compiles is almost unbelievable.

The picture that stays in your mind will happen in time.

In Mark 5, the sick woman said: "If I can touch the hem of His garment, I know I'll be healed." She had a *mental picture* of her effort...and the actual healing resulting.

When Abraham saw stars, he *visualized his children* to come. Jesus, for the joy that was set *before* Him, endured the cross. He pictured the resurrection, the ascension, the return to the Father...*it energized Him to endure the crucifixion.*

7.   Never Let Go In The Night What God Has Promised In The Light.

Miracles are for the *persistent,* not the wisher. Hold on to what God wants you to have. You are Heaven's favorite product. God's entire promotional program is geared to *you.* The book of Ephesians says that you are *chosen,* you are *blessed,* you are *predestinated,* you are *accepted,* you are *quickened,* you are *seated* in Heavenly places. "Blessed be the God and Father of our Lord Jesus Christ, Who hath blessed us with all spiritual blessings in heavenly places in Christ: Having predestinated us unto the adoption of children by Jesus Christ to Himself, according to the good pleasure of His will, To the praise of the glory of His grace, wherein He hath made us accepted in the Beloved. In Whom we have redemption through His blood, the forgiveness of sins, according to the riches of His grace; Wherein He hath abounded toward us in all wisdom and prudence;" (Ephesians 1:3,5-8).

God established the miracle-system. He wants it to work for *you*. Go ahead...reach for your miracle!

You were born to taste the Grapes!

≈ 22 ≈

THE SECRETS BEHIND SUCCESSFUL PRAYING

Prayer Is Your Greatest Weapon.

Champions always use it against satanic pressures. It is a subject talked about...preached about...written about....but usually it is not really practiced. Few people grasp prayer's incredible potential.

Prayer is visiting with your Father.

Jesus, as your example, often communicated with God through prayer. He knew it was the only way to truly win over sickness or the power of demonic spirits. It built His relationship with His Father.

Prayer puts fear in the heart of satan, your adversary.

God *expects* it.

Angels *respect* it.

It is the most powerful way to change the destiny of your life.

I believe prayer is the only pathway to true peace and daily strength. In this chapter, I have listed the questions most frequently asked about it.

Why Should We Pray?

First, God *Commanded* It. "And He spake a

parable unto them to this end, that men ought always to pray, and not to faint;" (Luke 18:1). In His words, we are to "always" pray. He expects it daily.

Second, Prayer Is Your *Key* To *Power*. Read carefully this unforgettable passage in Acts 12.

"Peter therefore was kept in prison: but prayer was made without ceasing of the church unto God for him.

"And when Herod would have brought him forth, the same night Peter was sleeping between two soldiers, bound with two chains: and the keepers before the door kept the prison.

"And, behold, the angel of the Lord came upon him, and a light shined in the prison: and he smote Peter on the side, and raised him up, saying, Arise up quickly. And his chains fell off from his hands.

"And the angel said unto him, Gird thyself, and bind on thy sandals. And so he did. And he saith unto him, Cast thy garment about thee, and follow me.

"And he went out, and followed him; and wist not that it was true which was done by the angel; but thought he saw a vision.

"When they were past the first and the second ward, they came unto the iron gate that leadeth unto the city; which opened to them of his own accord: and they went out, and passed on through one street; and forthwith the angel departed from him.

"And when Peter was come to himself, he said, Now I know of a surety, that the Lord hath sent His angel, and hath delivered me out of the hand of Herod, and from all the expectation of the people of the Jews.

"And when he had considered the thing, he came to the house of Mary the mother of John, whose surname was Mark; where many were gathered together praying.

"And as Peter knocked at the door of the gate, a damsel came to hearken, named Rhoda.

"And when she knew Peter's voice, she opened not the gate for gladness, but ran in, and told how Peter stood before the gate.

"And they said unto her, Thou art mad. But she constantly affirmed that it was even so. Then said they, It is his angel.

"But Peter continued knocking: and when they had opened the door, and saw him, they were astonished.

"But he, beckoning unto them with the hand to hold their peace, declared unto them how the Lord had brought him out of the prison. And he said, Go shew these things unto James, and to the brethren. And he departed, and went into another place" (Acts 12:5-17).

It gives you, the believer, *authority* over satan.

What Does Prayer Do?

Prayer changes your "*inner* world." The peace and presence of God fills you. It also changes your *external* circumstances: The hand of God moves people around you and miracles begin to happen.

1.   **Prayer Pleasures *The Heart Of God.***
"And there I will meet with thee, and I will commune with thee from above the mercy seat, from between the two cherubims which are upon the ark of the testimony, of all things which I will give thee in

commandment unto the children of Israel" (Exodus 25:22).

God enjoys your companionship.

He seeks communion with you.

2. **Prayer Pleasures *You*.** "Come unto Me, all ye that labour and are heavy laden, and I will give you rest" (Matthew 11:28). When you pray, your spirit is fed the essential "bread of life." Prayer is as necessary for your spirit as food is for your body.

3. **Prayer Blesses *Others*.** "I exhort therefore, that, first of all, supplications, prayers, intercessions, and giving of thanks, be made for all men;" (1 Timothy 2:1).

When you lift others and their needs before God, not only will their needs be met, but yours will be satisfied also. "And the Lord turned the captivity of Job, when he prayed for his friends: also the Lord gave Job twice as much as he had before" (Job 42:10).

4. **Prayer Opens The Door For God To Show Us Great And Mighty Things.** "Call unto Me, and I will answer thee, and shew thee great and mighty things, which thou knowest not" (Jeremiah 33:3).

Where Should You Pray?

First, You Should Pray In *Public Worship And Praise Services* With Other Believers.

Second, You Should Pray In Your "Closet Of Prayers"...*Alone*. "And when He had sent the multitudes away, He went up into a mountain apart to pray: and when the evening was come, He was there alone:" (Matthew 14:23). "And He withdrew himself into the wilderness, and prayed" (Luke 5:16).

Jesus often prayed unaccompanied during the most critical times of His life.

He needed to be *alone* with His Father.

What Should You Pray About?

First, Your National Leaders And Heads Of State. You must focus prayer on the leaders of the world. "I exhort therefore, that, first of all, supplications, prayers, intercessions, and giving of thanks, be made for all men: For kings, and for all that are in authority; that we may lead a quiet and peaceable life in all godliness and honesty. For this is good and acceptable in the sight of God our Savior; Who will have all men to be saved, and to come unto the knowledge of the truth" (1 Timothy 2:1-4).

Second, Other Countries. You should lift up other nations before God. Many of them do not have the freedom of prayer without fear of persecution— or even death.

Third, Unbelievers Who Are Lost And Dying Without Jesus Christ. "Ask of Me, and I shall give thee the heathen for thine inheritance, and the uttermost parts of the earth for thy possession" (Psalm 2:8).

Fourth, Laborers To Gather In Souls Of The Harvest. "Then saith He unto His disciples, The harvest truly is plenteous, but the labourers are few; Pray ye therefore the Lord of the harvest, that He will send forth labourers into His harvest" (Matthew 9:37,38).

Fifth, World Revival. Our churches need to be restored to their original consciousness of holy living and world evangelism. Many of them have long since forgotten their purpose for being.

Sixth, New Converts. As a believer established in the Word, you should remember new converts in prayer, those at home and especially those in other nations.

2 Tragedies That Happen When You Refuse To Pray

1.   **There Is An Absence Of *Results*.** Satanic forces are unrestrained without prayer and confession of the Word.

2.   **There Is An Absence Of *Purification*.** Prayer forces the carnal nature into the presence of a Holy God. It is impossible to walk in hourly obedience without a strong personal prayer life.

5 Hindrances To Your Prayer Life

1.   **Your Failure To Recognize Your Right As A Child Of God.**

2.   **Your Ignorance Of The Power Of Prayer.**

3.   **Your Laziness And Apathy.** It takes discipline to get alone with God.

4.   **Your Attitude.** Negative attitudes in praying prevent your receiving the answer. You should always pray the "promise," instead of your problem.

5.   **Your Feelings.** If you pray only when you feel like it—you will probably seldom pray.

7 Reasons For Unanswered Prayer

1.   **Wrong Motive.**

"Ye ask, and receive not, because ye ask amiss, that ye may consume it upon your lusts" (James 4:3).

2.   Sin In Your Heart.

"Behold, the Lord's hand is not shortened, that it cannot save; neither His ear heavy, that it cannot hear: But your iniquities have separated between you and your God, and your sins have hid His face from you, that He will not hear" (Isaiah 59:1,2).

3.   Idols In Your Life.

"Then came certain of the elders of Israel unto me, and sat before me. And the word of the Lord came unto me, saying, Son of man, these men have set up their idols in their heart, and put the stumblingblock of their iniquity before their face: should I be enquired of at all by them?" (Ezekiel 14:1-3).

4.   An Unforgiving Spirit.

"And when ye stand praying, forgive, if ye have ought against any: that your Father also which is in heaven may forgive you your trespasses" (Mark 11:25).

5.   A Lack Of Generosity.

"Whoso stoppeth his ears at the cry of the poor, he also shall cry himself, but shall not be heard" (Proverbs 21:13).

6.   Mistreatment Of Your Family Members.

"Likewise, ye husbands, dwell with them according to knowledge, giving honour unto the wife, as unto the weaker vessel, and as being heirs together of the grace of life; that your prayers be not hindered" (1 Peter 3:7).

7.   Your Lack Of Faith.

"Then touched He their eyes, saying, According to your faith be it unto you" (Matthew 9:29).

7 Keys To Answered Prayers

There are laws for successful praying. They work, *when you apply them*. If you ignore them, your prayers will be ineffective and a waste of time. What are these important essentials in *your prayer life?*

1.   You Must Pray To The Father.

"And in that day ye shall ask me nothing. Verily, verily, I say unto you, Whatsoever ye shall ask the Father in my name, He will give it you" (John 16:23).

2.   You Must Pray In The Name Of Jesus.

"Verily, verily, I say unto you, He that believeth on Me, the works that I do shall he do also; and greater works than these shall he do; because I go unto My Father. And whatsoever ye shall ask in My name, that will I do, that the Father may be glorified in the Son. If ye shall ask any thing in My name, I will do it. If ye love Me, keep My commandments" (John 14:12-15).

3.   You Must Pray By The Holy Spirit.

"Likewise the Spirit also helpeth our infirmities; for we know not what we should pray for as we ought: but the Spirit itself maketh intercession for us with groanings which cannot be uttered" (Romans 8:26).

4.   You Must Pray With Full Understanding Of Your Rights And Privileges.

"For if I pray in an unknown tongue, my Spirit prayeth, but my understanding is unfruitful. What is it then? I will pray with the Spirit, and I will pray with the understanding also: I will sing with the

Spirit, and I will sing with the understanding also:" (1 Corinthians 14:14,15).

5. You Must Pray In Harmony With The Word Of God.

"If ye abide in Me, and My words abide in you, ye shall ask what ye will, and it shall be done unto you" (John 15:7).

6. You Must Pray In Faith, Doubting Nothing.

"But let him ask in faith, nothing wavering. For he that wavereth is like a wave of the sea driven with the wind and tossed" (James 1:6).

7. You Must Pray With Praise For The Answer.

"Be careful for nothing; but in every thing by prayer and supplication with thanksgiving let your requests be made known unto God" (Philippians 4:6).

5 Important Prayer Habits

Here are some essentials in helping you develop your morning prayer time with God.

1. You Should Establish A Definite Morning Prayer Time.

2. You Should Establish A Definite Place.

3. You Should Talk To God Immediately Upon Rising.

4. You Should Establish A Prayer List And Keep It Current.

5. You Should Learn To Pray Aloud.

I know there are many believers who want to walk in power, who want to live as overcomers, who long to break off habits in their lives...*but have never learned the truth about power prayer.* They *want* to become disciplined. They *want* to develop a time and place—but *never started.*

Start today!

Start this very minute praying aloud. Learn to activate the climate around you with praise...power ...and thanksgiving!

He who succeeds in his prayer life...succeeds in life.

He who fails in his prayer life...fails in life.

✿ 23 ✿

HOW TO READ AND UNDERSTAND THE BIBLE

1. Be Persuaded Of The Importance Of Reading The Word Of God Habitually.

It is like food for your body, something you need regularly. However, it is mind-food and spirit-food. You may not sense its effect upon you *immediately*. If we could taste it like we do the sirloin steak, we would dive in hourly! However, the full impact of exposing the mind to the Word is usually *progressive*.

The Word *exposes your mind to the mentality of God*. Your heart is in the climate of truth. You are *programming* into your spirit, the very heart of God.

2. Concentrate On These Ten Promised Results Of The Word.

▶ It will bring *cleansing*. "Wherewithal shall a young man cleanse his way? by taking heed thereto according to Thy Word" (Psalm 119:9). "Now ye are clean through the Word which I have spoken unto you" (John 15:3).

▶ It will build *faith*. "So then faith cometh by hearing, and hearing by the Word of God" (Romans 10:17).

▶ It will give *power* to *resist* sin. "Thy Word have I hid in mine heart, that I might not sin against Thee. My soul melteth for heaviness: strengthen Thou me according unto Thy Word. Unless Thy law had been my delights, I should then have perished in mine affliction" (Psalm 119:11,28,92).

▶ It will give *victory* and a happy life. "The statutes of the Lord are right, rejoicing the heart: the commandment of the Lord is pure, enlightening the eyes. Thy Word have I hid in mine heart, that I might not sin against Thee" (Psalm 19:8; 119:11).

▶ It will provide *discernment*. "Thy Word is a lamp unto my feet, and a light unto my path. The entrance of Thy words giveth light; it giveth understanding unto the simple" (Psalm 119:105,130).

▶ It will give *comfort* during pressure times. "Remember the Word unto Thy servant, upon which Thou hast caused me to hope. This is my comfort in my affliction: for Thy Word hath quickened me:" (Psalm 119:49,50).

▶ It will provide *correction* and *reveal truth*. "All Scripture is given by inspiration of God, and is profitable for doctrine, for reproof, for correction, for instruction in righteousness" (2 Timothy 3:16). "The statutes of the Lord are right, rejoicing the heart: the commandment of the Lord is pure, enlightening the eyes" (Psalm 19:8).

▶ It will give *warning*. "Moreover by them is Thy servant warned: and in keeping of them there is great reward" (Psalm 19:11).

▶ It will build *stability.* "The law of his God is in his heart: none of his steps shall slide" (Psalm 37:31).

▶ It will give *peace of mind.* "Great peace have they which love Thy law: and nothing shall offend them" (Psalm 119:165). "And the work of righteousness shall be peace; and the effect of righteousness quietness and assurance for ever" (Isaiah 32:17). "For length of days, and long life, and peace, shall they add to thee" (Proverbs 3:2).

These are just a few of the many benefits. Without the *continuous* entrance of the Word, you will *lack* all of the above qualities.

3.   Quit Condemning Yourself And Carefully Begin Building The Bible Habit.

Satan fights your reading the Bible because of the power he knows you will develop as you read it. He will not oppose the reading of newspapers and novels. The opposition you feel as you attempt to read the Word is unseen, satanic and devised to rob you of the Word's power and benefits. Once you develop the ability to at least begin reading each morning, the Holy Spirit reinforces that *decision and act* and you will find yourself *not wanting to quit!*

> **WISDOM PRINCIPLE 60**
>
> *When You Get Into The Word — The Word Will Get Into You.*

4.   Create And Control The Climate For Your Reading Time.

▶ Choose a specific *place,* and a definite

time. (If sleep habits vary, just plan to begin your reading within the first hour of the day.)

▶ Select a *system.* Do not always read at random. Sometimes read from Genesis through Revelation. Or choose one book in the New Testament and read it over and over. Or, you may want to pursue one particular subject each month. This is half the battle! Know *where* you are going to be reading.

▶ Read with a specific *purpose.* Ask yourself: "What does this reveal about God, people or me?"

▶ *Select* a Bible that is easy and enjoyable to read. Large print Bibles often make it easier for many readers.

▶ *Write* down what you learn.

▶ Read the Bible *aloud* as a prayer or statement of faith to God—it's powerful!

5. Begin Today.

You will not "wake-up" to an easier time. *Start* this very day. *Talk* to others *about the truths* you have read today.

Don't get uptight about remembering it all. It will come back to you when necessary...*just get into the Word, and the Word will get into you.* You might want to keep a daily schedule. Your local Christian bookstore will have many good helps along this line.

Your attachment to the Word of God affects your attitude, your happiness and the joy of your achievements.

☞ 24 ☜

GOD'S GOLDEN KEY TO YOUR SUCCESS

God wants you successful!

Are you shocked by this statement? Thousands of people throughout the world are experiencing a revolution in their lives. Spiritual rebirth, physical healings, financial miracles are happening to people just like you! People are seeing *what God is really like,* and this photograph is igniting a fire of excitement like they have never experienced before.

Everything God can do was meant to happen to you!

3 Important Keys

1.   You Have Worth. Everything God creates has tremendous value. This makes you the object of God's attention and affection. Your life can be changed just by understanding these explosive truths.

2.   God Created You. He made you in His image, after His form and likeness. The Bible teaches that you and I are God's highest creation. Man was given dominion over everything else God made, over the earth and all its inhabitants.

3.   God Placed At Your Disposal An Unlimited Wealth Of Resources. As the owner of everything in the universe, God intended that His people should not lack for anything. He intended that man should know how to make full use of every resource. So, He implanted within you the "Seeds for Success" in every area of your life. As His supreme creation, God poured into you His mind, His power, His sensitivity, His Wisdom — *everything necessary for us to succeed.*

Your success is always on God's mind. Very early in the Word of God it is established that success and prosperity are worthy and worthwhile goals for man in God's eyes, In Joshua 1:7-8 we read: "Only be thou strong and very courageous, that thou mayest observe to do according to all the law, which Moses My servant commanded thee: turn not from it to the right hand or to the left, that thou mayest prosper whithersoever thou goest. This book of the law shall not depart out of thy mouth; but thou shalt meditate therein day and night, that thou mayest observe to do according to all that is written therein: for then thou shalt make thy way prosperous, and then thou shalt have good success."

These verses are highly significant. They establish in no uncertain terms that God wants you successful and to enjoy prosperity. God's will is that *"thou mayest prosper withersoever thou goest."*

As you follow His divine Formulas for Success taught in the Word of God, *"then thou shalt make thy way prosperous, and then thou shalt have good success."*

There is no mistaking what the Bible says. Either you believe the Word of God, or you don't. If you accept the Bible as being true, then you must believe God wants His children to be successful.

3 Reasons God Wants You To Succeed!

1. Your Life Is On Display.

God wants your success to serve as an example of what His love and power can do in a person's life. By sending success into the lives of His children, God can demonstrate to an unbelieving world both His nature and His power. The apostle Paul wrote: "...God hath chosen the weak things of the world to confound the things which are mighty;" (1 Corinthians 1:27). He also testified that God dealt with him and said: "...my strength is made perfect in weakness" (2 Corinthians 12:9).

Have you ever known people who seemed to be the model of success in every area of life—spiritually, physically and mentally? Their life appeared almost perfect. Their financial condition was stable. Their family and social life was an example of all that is wholesome, healthy and desirable.

Yet, as you studied those individuals, you found it hard to pinpoint the secret of their success. Do you know what I mean? There seemed to be no outstanding abilities or resources within these people for them to draw from. Maybe you have looked at people like this and wondered what their real secret was.

The Master Key to any truly successful life is Daily Obedience.

For instance, Abraham's *obedience* brought the blessings of God in abundance. He served as an example to each of us of what God wants for His children. "And if ye be Christ's, then are ye Abraham's seed, and heirs according to the promise" (Galatians 3:29).

2.   To Provide For Your Family.

God wants to give you success to enable you to provide for your family needs. The Bible makes it explicitly clear that we must provide for the material as well as the spiritual elders: "But if any provide not for his own, and specially for those of his own house, he hath denied the faith, and is worse than an infidel" (1 Timothy 5:8). God gets no glory if your family has to live in a rat-breeding, roach-infested tenement. He is not pleased if your family never has enough to eat, and your children wear "hand-me-downs" and go without shoes. He is a God of abundance of blessings. He wants you and your family to have plenty...and to spare.

3.   To Carry Out The Great Commission.

The third reason God wants you successful is to financially support and undergird the *work of God*. As God sends prosperity into your life, He not only meets your needs, but also makes it possible for you to help carry out the Great Commission. Someone has said that money in the hands of an unbeliever is a *snare,* but money in the hands of a believer is a *tool* to do God's will...to carry out the Great Commission.

As Christians are prospered financially and use their resources for God's work, good things start happening. Churches are built, mission stations are established, gospel radio and television programs are aired, soul winning ministries are launched to share the message of salvation with those who have not yet been born again. All these things cost money. So God prospers His people that there will be no shortage of funds to do His work.

Thousands of people have misunderstood God's attitude toward success and prosperity. Somewhere they have gotten the idea that it is wrong to want to be successful. In fact, some even feel that prosperity is of the devil. Nothing could be further from the truth! Don't be misled. God *does* want you successful! His Word *does* say: "...thou shalt make thy way prosperous, and then thou shalt have good success" (Joshua 1:8).

What Is Success?

When you say the word *success,* everybody thinks of yachts, gorgeous homes, big cars, fancy clothes and huge bank accounts. It is quite possible to have all these possessions and be successful. Unfortunately, merely having these possessions does not necessarily make a person successful. Many who possess all of this have honestly admitted openly that they are still unhappy with their lives.

Some people define success in terms of power, position, prestige and popularity. Again, the successful person may enjoy all these things, but even these attributes are not, in themselves, the foundation stones of success.

Still others say that success is achieving the goals you set for yourself. The question is, does the attainment of those particular goals produce genuine satisfaction in the heart, the *inner world?* The *external* picture of success does not necessarily guarantee *internal* happiness.

I remember reading in history about Alexander the Great. He went out with his armies to conquer the nations of the world. After the last victorious battle had ended, it is said Alexander wept because there were no more worlds left for him to conquer! He achieved all his goals but did not find abiding satisfaction and happiness.

Real Success

If success is not measured in terms of possessions, popularity and performance, how then can it be defined? Perhaps the simplest definition of success for the believer is *knowing and attaining God's goals for your life.* A successful life is one that is happy.

Becoming what God wants you to become.

Doing what God wants you to do.

Possessing what God wants you to own.

As you achieve the goals *God* has set for your life, then you become successful. Someone once said, "Success is not merely getting what you want, but wanting what you got after you get it." Some fellow may throw away all he has to win the heart of a certain girl, only to discover later her greatest talent is making him miserable! *He got what he wanted, but didn't want what he got.*

In their quest for achievement, some people become so greedy and grasping they are *never* satisfied with *any* accomplishment. They never enjoy what God has *already* given them.

Real success is not a destination, it is a journey. It is movement. It is the joy created by *progress.* Success is not a city where you will arrive *tomorrow,* it is the enjoyment of today, *the now.* Every person is somewhere on God's maturity schedule, from "A" to "Z." Real success is keeping the schedule God has for you and His Assignment for your life.

Stay On God's Schedule For Success

What does all this mean? Simply that success means different things to different people, depending on where they are on God's maturity schedule. If someone offered a baby the keys to a new car, it would mean very little to him. He wants his bottle of milk! Having the keys to his own automobile would not be success to him. Being given his bottle and a soft pillow for his head is the best thing that could happen to him right now.

However, if that baby continued to progress along God's maturity schedule, about 16 years later, if he were offered a baby bottle and a soft pillow, he would be very disappointed. It would not be his idea of the ideal way to spend an evening. That's the time he is interested in the offer of the keys to the car!

That's why I say *true success is achieving the goals God presently has for you.* Some Christians have stopped along God's maturity schedule at about letter "C." Instead of realizing God wants them to prosper and be successful, they sit back with a "baby bottle" and wonder why they find very little satisfaction in life.

On the other hand, it is possible to try to get too far *ahead* of God's schedule. I know some people who are trying to achieve level "S" or "T" when they should be back on about "M." Because of their misdirected attention focus, they are completely dissatisfied with the achievements they are making on their present level.

Remember, *success is different things to different*

people at different times. Find out where you are on your journey. Learn to enjoy what you are already receiving instead of being unhappy because you haven't got everything you are wanting.

One man I know thought his "success goal" was a lot of money. You can imagine how he felt when he read in the newspaper about a guy who won a contest and was awarded the prize of $100,000. "Wow, what a lucky guy," the man said. "Nothing could make me unhappy if I could win $100,000 like he did!"

Then my friend read the next paragraph of the news story. He learned that the "winner" was a prisoner on death row, scheduled to be electrocuted in a short time. From the prisoner's point of view, the $100,000 prize didn't spell success. The money wasn't going to do him much good!

Never forget that being successful is achieving the *goals* God has for you in *every* area of your life. What are these areas? God has a success plan for you *spiritually, physically, emotionally, financially, socially* and in your *family life.* And He has provided a Golden Key to help you unlock the Doors of Success in every single area.

Success is the achievement of the goals God has for you!

God's Golden Key

When I was growing up, all the kids in the neighborhood would gather around to talk. One of our favorite topics was the "one-wish game." Someone would say, "If you could have anything in the whole world, what one thing would you wish for?"

The girls usually wanted a date with some popular guy at school. The fellow down the block wished for a motorcycle. A teenager who was having problems at home might say he wished he had no parents! One girl wished she had $1,000 to spend on new clothes.

Everyone in the group always had one or two things to wish for. Every time we played the game there always was something each youngster either wanted to have or wished to avoid. Of course, there was no one listening to our wishes who had the power to grant them. One day a new boy in our neighborhood stunned us all by his statement of his one wish, "I wish for one thing—the *wishing ability* that anything I wish for would come true." Naturally, for such clever thinking he became our leading local genius!

There is a story in the Bible, though, of a man who was actually guaranteed that he would be given anything he asked for: "...the Lord appeared to Solomon in a dream by night: and God said, Ask what I shall give thee" (1 Kings 3:5).

What a dramatic situation! It was as if God had led Solomon to the front of a great hotel and said, "Choose any room you want, and you can have it. One room has *riches* inside. Another has *long life*. One room has *power and authority*. Each room contains something desirable—something you would like to have. Just tell me which room you want most and I will give you the key to it."

Solomon thought about God's offer for a moment. Then he said quietly, "Give me the key to the room which contains Wisdom and understanding."

God smiled, and opened up the ring of keys in

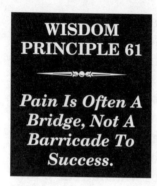

WISDOM PRINCIPLE 61

Pain Is Often A Bridge, Not A Barricade To Success.

His hand. He took off a golden key and handed it to Solomon. "You have made a wise choice," He said.

Solomon asked, "Why is this key different from all the rest?"

"Because this is the *Master Key* it will unlock *all the rooms* in the entire building!"

Yes, *Understanding is God's Golden Key to your success. Understanding!* At first it sounds like nothing. It seems trite and meaningless. But *Understanding* the *Master Key* that opens the doors of opportunity to you and gives you free access to every resource. *Understanding* unlocks the doors to all your goals, ambitions and desires. *Understanding* will smash the locks on your prison of prejudices, fears and unhappiness!

What Is Understanding?

Understanding is the sum total of both knowledge and Wisdom. *It is the ability to interpret life as God sees it — the ability to see the total picture that God sees of a person or a situation.* Understanding is the ability:

▶ To *see* through His eyes,
▶ To *hear* through His ears,
▶ To *feel* as with His heart,
▶ To *walk* in His steps,
▶ To *think* with His mind.

No marriage would ever be destroyed by divorce if the husband saw his wife *through the eyes of God,* and the wife could see her husband *as God sees him.*

A man would be able to become wealthy almost overnight if he knew the hearts of people and all the details of business propositions as God knows them.

Parents and children would have no crushing conflicts if they dealt with each other from the standpoint of understanding. How many teenagers look at their parents and wish they could go pack their bags and leave home because nobody understands them? While they are thinking that, the parents' hearts are just aching: "Oh honey, if you could just see how we love you. If you could just know how we think and feel about you!"

The Golden Key of Understanding makes it possible for parents and children to communicate—to hear what the other is saying *with their heart.* Understanding will open the door to harmony and happiness in the home.

WISDOM PRINCIPLE 62

You Create A Season Of Success Every Time You Complete An Instruction From God.

Understanding is also *seeing God's purpose in some of life's more unpleasant events.* The Bible tells how Joseph was sold into slavery by his brothers. As a slave, he tried to do what was right and was the target of vicious lies as a result. He ended up in a dungeon. Through all this pain and persecution, Joseph maintained his faith in God. How? By being aware of God's hand at work in his behalf. Because he was in the dungeon *at the right*

194 ■ *MIKE MURDOCK*

time, he was given the *opportunity to minister* by interpreting Pharaoh's troubling dreams. *This catapulted him to power.* In a short time he had become Pharaoh's chief officer of the entire land. With God's direction he was able to prepare for a time of great famine in the land.

When the famine came, Joseph was able to save an entire nation. Plus, he was in a position to save the lives of his own family—including the brothers who had betrayed him. Understanding helped him to see *God's purpose* in his problems and make him successful.

By using the Golden Key to Understanding, we can unlock the doors of opportunity in every part of our life, even in our finances, and walk through them confidently to gain success. When you ask God for the Golden Key of Understanding, He says to you: "I am the Lord thy God which teacheth thee to profit, which leadeth thee by the way that thou shouldest go" (Isaiah 48:17).

$124,000 Profit In 30 Days!

A friend of mine was driving by a piece of property and suddenly he felt a strong impression that he should buy it. The selling price was $75,000, and my friend didn't have that kind of money. He couldn't see why he should buy such an expensive piece of ground that he didn't even need. But the voice of God kept speaking to him. *God knew something he didn't know and wanted to share it with him.*

My friend felt this leading of the Lord so strongly that he began scraping together what money he could. He took all of his savings out of the bank. He sold some items. He took all the cash he could get together and made a down payment on that piece of property.

Thirty days later he was on that lot, burning some trash and generally cleaning up a bit. A car drove up and a lady got out, walked over and asked if he was the owner. Then she wanted to know if the property was for sale.

When my friend assured her he was the owner, she said, "My husband is a doctor. He has been wanting to buy this land for four years. We're prepared to offer you $199,000 for this property."

In 30 days time, my friend was offered a $124,000 profit! He was able to achieve this remarkable success—not in his own Wisdom, but through the Divine Understanding of God—*the ability to see the picture of that property as God saw it. His obedience created the miracle.*

What God did for this man, He will do for *you.* God is no respecter of persons. His promises are for everybody. He has a Golden Key of Understanding waiting for you.

Where Does Understanding Come From?

All Understanding comes from God. It is a gift *only God can give.* That is why Solomon had to ask for Understanding instead of trying to rely upon himself. God bestows Understanding upon us through His Word: "For the Lord giveth wisdom: out of His mouth cometh knowledge and understanding" (Proverbs 2:6). The Psalmist said of God: "Through Thy precepts I get understanding:" (Psalm 119:104).

So the Word of God opens up understanding to us. The entire Bible was written that you and I would have Understanding—that we would be able to interpret life as God does. Paul, one of the prolific writers of the New Testament, said: "Consider what I say; and the Lord give thee understanding in all things" (2 Timothy 2:7).

By carefully reading the Word of God, we learn to use the Golden Key of Understanding in unlocking the Doors of Success. As we immerse ourselves in the Bible, God speaks to us from His Word and says, "This is what I *think*. This is what I *know*. This is what I *see*. This is what I *hear*."

God has breathed His divine knowledge into the Word. *Between the covers of your Bible are the treasures you need to be truly successful.* You will find the answer to financial troubles, how to cure worry, even how to solve friendship problems. The Word will direct you in your *family* relationships— the chain of authority in the home, including the position of the husband, the wife and the children.

The Bible contains a cure for nervousness and depression. The Word is even the purging tool for removing immorality from our minds and lives: "Wherewithal shall a young man cleanse his way? by taking heed thereto according to Thy Word" (Psalm 119:9).

So, *the Bible is the success book of the world!* It is the source of God's Golden Key for Success: "The entrance of Thy Words giveth light; it giveth understanding unto the simple" (Psalm 119:130).

An interesting note is that one of the most important functions of the Holy Spirit is to *interpret* the Word of God to believers and *produce* understanding. This means when we come across a passage of scripture that is not clear to us, the Holy Spirit enlightens our minds and makes every detail sharp and meaningful: "Howbeit when He, the Spirit of truth, is come, He will guide you into all truth:" (John 16:13). It was this Spirit that rested upon Jesus as Isaiah prophesied: "And the Spirit of the Lord shall rest upon him, the Spirit of wisdom and understanding," (Isaiah 11:2). But we must desire and *ask* for this Wisdom. If we will do that, God will give it to us *liberally* according to James 1:5.

Your Study Program For Success

Your regularity in Bible study is vitally important. It helps unfold God's total requirements for success through enlightenment and understanding. As you delve into the rich Wisdom of the Bible, you will come to understand *God, others and yourself.* **First, As You Learn The Truth About *God* And Find Out About His Nature, His Opinions, And His Sense Of Values, You Experience The Thrill Of Discovering *Where* He Wants You, *When* He Wants You There, And *How* He Chooses To Place You There.**

Second, The Bible Enables You To See *Others* As God Sees Them. You begin to understand their place in your life. You learn to recognize and anticipate their needs and the part God wants you to have in ministering to them.

Third, God's Word Helps You Come To A Better Understanding Of *Yourself.* You begin to catch a glimpse of the importance God places on *you.* You start to interpret yourself *as God sees you,* both now and potentially. You will see more than your problems. You will begin to see the *possibilities* God sees in you.

To receive God's Golden Key—Understanding— establish *regular* Bible study habits. Start consuming the Word of God. The best advice I can offer you is to set a *definite daily study time.* Spend part of that time just reading—not trying to delve deeply into complex theological concepts. Simply *read* what God has to say and let the Word speak to your heart.

Maybe you would enjoy selecting one subject that appeals to you to study further and become an expert in that specific topic. Perhaps you are interested in *angels* or *healing* or *prophecy. Begin to become a Bible expert on that particular subject.* Bible helps, concordances, commentaries and other research material will enable you to find everything the Bible has to say and to compare opinions of other scholars about the subject you have chosen. This will give you *confidence* in your knowledge of the Word. Also, be sure the Bible you use has easy-to-read type and is a comfortable size.

Learning The Way Of The Winner

Keep in mind *always* that the Bible is a Book of Success. It tells you about people's successes and failures. It is literally the book that shows you the "Way of the Winner."

The Word of God outlines how you can be a *victor* instead of a *victim*—how you can win instead of lose. It teaches you to have a *Sonship mentality* instead of a *slave mentality.*

The Bible tells you *how to think*. It shows *what* influences you. It outlines everything you need to know about *God*, everything you need to know about *yourself*, and everything you need to know about *people and their behavior.*

Last, but certainly not least, the Word of God can make you *happy*. One of the side benefits of success is happiness. The Bible says: "Happy is the man that findeth wisdom, and the man that getteth understanding" (Proverbs 3:13).

So, now you know where Understanding comes from, and how to go about finding success and happiness through the Word of God. Don't let anything stop you from using this key to open up a whole new world for yourself. Satan will try to divert you, distract you, interrupt you—anything to keep you from finding the success he knows the Bible will open up for you. Keep to your purpose. As the Word begins to come alive in you, your desire and appetite for the Bible will increase. You will be well on your way to habitual victory.

God's Word is the Key to success and happiness. Use this Key every day!

Develop A New Picture Of Yourself

The Bible is the original Book of Success. It is a book of *pictures*. It gives you a picture of *God*. It gives you a picture of *yourself*. It gives you a picture of *others*. In the Bible you can see a picture of Abraham and his success. You can see a picture of Joseph and his success. You can even see pictures of people like Elijah, Jonah and Paul in moments of stress, and also in moments of triumph. As you become more and more familiar with the Word of God, you build into the gallery of your mind a collection of photographs of the success stories of the Bible.

As you study these pictures, you will soon discover another image beginning to take shape. You will recognize this as a picture of you. You begin to see yourself, not as what you have been, but as *what you are going to be.* You see yourself, not where you have been, but *where you are going.* You see a picture, not of what you have done, *but of what you are going to do.* This fresh mental picture of yourself should become your goal. Through daily Scripture intake you can reinforce that picture of yourself, *as God sees you.*

> **WISDOM PRINCIPLE 63**
>
> *You Will Always Struggle, Subconsciously To Become The Self-Portrait You Believe Yourself To Be.*

Your own destiny can be determined by the way you see yourself. Never permit yourself to say, "I'm stupid. I'm dumb. I'm a failure."

Instead, see yourself as mentally sharp, brilliant, a *Winner.* Why? Because you have access to the mind of God. The Bible says: "Let this mind be in you, which was also in Christ Jesus: Who, being in the form of God, thought it not robbery to be equal with God:" (Philippians 2:5,6).

Your Self-Portrait

When you see yourself with the mind of Christ,

you see a portrait of success—a picture that has been retouched to take out the blemishes of failure and the wrinkles of weakness. What remains is the perfect likeness of a Winner—and *that is the way God sees you.* He has a marvelous and thrilling photograph album of you. He sees all of your high points, good qualities and positive attributes.

Satan will try to show you a photograph of yourself at your *worst.* He tries to remind you of what you were like at your weakest point. He takes a photograph of you when you were down and out and that's what he holds in front of your face all the time. He even puts a magnifying glass in front of your defects and says, "Look how bad you look...how ugly you are!" His whole purpose is to give you a different image of yourself than what God sees in you.

So many people spend all their time looking at failure photographs of themselves and trying to cover up what is really a distorted picture. Problems between people sometimes start when we start exchanging these ugly photographs of each other. A wife looks at her husband and says, "I can't stand how disorganized you are, leaving your clothes on the floor. I'm tired of picking up after you."

He replies, "Well, look at how lazy you are. You never keep the dishes washed. You have not cooked in a week! I'm tired of coming home to a dirty house!"

People go around trading photographs of one another at their worst... instead of talking about the good pictures, the strong points. And as long as they do that, they keep right on being failures.

But the moment they begin to see themselves

as God sees them, 90 percent of their pressure areas and problem areas are released. Because if they can see themselves through the eyes of God, they start concentrating on their *potential,* not their problems.

The Success Maker

Jesus came to make men successful. He is the original Success-Maker. He came to upgrade men and women, and yes, even teenagers and children. God made you in His image. *You are important and valuable to Him.* You are an extension of His life and personality. You can be *like* Him. That's the way He meant for you to be.

"But what is God like?" Most of us have a very muddled, vague, hazy opinion of who God is. I heard about a mother who came upon her little boy busily drawing and coloring in his tablet. "What are you drawing, son?" she asked.

"A picture of God," he said.

"But Billy, nobody knows what God looks like," she told him.

The youngster thought about it a moment, then announced matter-of-factly: "They will when I get through." Oh, how I wish every minister of the gospel succeeded with that goal! It's so hard to explain beauty in a world that is often ugly and destructive. *God is a good God.*

Jesus came to show us what God is like. He said: "...he that hath seen Me hath seen the Father; (John 14:9). His whole purpose was to make you successful and show you what you are capable of *becoming...* of *doing...* of *possessing.*

Take a look at the life of Jesus. He proved His

power as a Success-Maker. He devoted His entire earthly ministry and life to helping people become more than they were and to have more than they had.

When Jesus saw people who were lonely, He spent time with them and had fellowship with them.

When Jesus saw people who were sick, *He healed them.*

When Jesus saw people who were eager to know more about God and life, *He taught them.*

When Jesus saw people who were hungry and faint, *He fed them.*

When Jesus saw people who were timid or bound by mediocrity, *He challenged them* to step out, stand up, launch out.

Jesus understood people, because He saw them *through the eyes of His Father.* That's why He could make them successful. For understanding is God's Golden Key to Success. Jesus understood the *needs* of the people, and *met those needs* in such a way as to make them successful. The Key to their success was Understanding—developing a new picture of themselves in God's image.

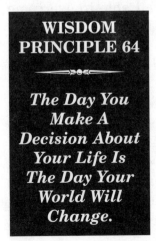

WISDOM PRINCIPLE 64

The Day You Make A Decision About Your Life Is The Day Your World Will Change.

The picture you develop for yourself is crucial to your success or failure. God wants you to see yourself as His highest creation. He is pouring *His mind* into you. He is pouring *His power* into you. He is pouring *His sensitivity* and *His Wisdom* into your life.

Overcoming The Slave Mentality

The Bible tells about the Israelites who were led out of bondage by Moses. This generation of Israelites were the descendants of people who had been slaves for 400 years. They had developed a *slave-mentality*. They saw themselves as put down. They were totally dominated by others. *They functioned best when someone told them what to do.* For generations life had been made to happen for them, so they did not know how to make life happen for themselves. They were not decision makers.

When these people approached the Promised Land, their leader sent 12 spies to scout out the land. Ten of them came back and said, "The inhabitants of the land are giants. We are like grasshoppers to them."

But two of the spies—Joshua and Caleb—had been able to find God's Golden Key to Success— Understanding. They knew God was with them and would make them victorious in any battle. So they reported, "The inhabitants of the land are like grasshoppers to us. We are well able to overcome them."

Joshua and Caleb had the ability to interpret the situation *from God's vantage point.* This capability spelled the difference between success and failure, between victory and defeat, between life and death.

And this one secret can transform your life and change your world. *Look at every situation from a higher viewpoint than your own.* Draw on your increasing supply of Understanding. Through faith, *begin to see through God's eyes.* Stop looking at

WISDOM PRINCIPLE 65

Your Harvest Will Always Come Through The Door Of Someone In Trouble, Who Is Needing Your Help.

the devil's picture of defeat and concentrate on God's portrait of prosperity and success.

This is your ticket to the "promised land" of your own personal success. Begin speaking aloud what you desire, not what you dread. *Speak your expectations*, not your fears. As God's child, begin developing the Sonship mentality. *Talk* it. *Think* it. *Accept and believe it.* You are God's property, and that relationship makes all the difference in the world in what happens to you. See yourself as God sees you—you are *His* property!

Some years ago something happened to me that literally changed the course of my life. It revolutionized my ministry. It transformed me. It made me a whole different person.

I was out in the garage that I had made into a makeshift office. I had been working for hours trying to catch up with some of my mail, filling orders, studying, writing, praying. I had been fasting five days. On the fifth day at 2:30 a.m., God spoke to my heart. Not aloud, but into my very spirit and innermost being. It was a simple sentence, but it struck me with the force of a sledgehammer blow. It echoed and resounded inside my head and engraved itself on the very walls of my heart. What was the message? Simply this, "What You Make Happen For Others, I Will Make Happen For You."

What You Make Happen For Others, God Will Make Happen For You.

I realized God was speaking to me. He burned this truth deep within my consciousness. Over and over those words came to me, and more and more I began to see this was the Golden Thread in the Garment of Life.

If I make good happen for others, God will make good happen for me. If I cause bad things to happen to others, bad things will happen to me. It works *both* ways. And it works *always,* without fail.

Now, all my life I had been taught that where I sowed, there would I reap. But the real truth is, *what* I sow, I will reap. Not *where* I sow. I may not reap from the same place I sow. God may have me sow Seeds in one person's field, and when Harvest time comes, I may reap from the field of someone else. Because the Source of my harvesting is not the caretaker of the field—but God, Who owns all.

What I make happen for others, God will make happen for me. That's the secret. That's the Understanding that becomes *your* key to success. Don't look for your Harvest *where* you have sowed. Look for your Harvest *because* you have sowed.

Create success situations for others around you. And don't be surprised or alarmed if they fail to return the favor. You sow in the lives of others, but your *expectation of return* is from God, your Heavenly Father, your Source.

So the basic law is very simple. If you want to be a success—if you want to be fulfilled—concentrate on the success and fulfillment of *others.* Get your mind off yourself. Quit talking about *your* needs and *your* desires. Think of ways to create success for the people around you. Help them reach *their* goals. Help them become fulfilled and happy.

Creating A Zone Of Success

What happens when you do this? When you make others successful, *you create a "zone" of success.* As you make the people around you successful, you are caught up in the middle of that success zone. And, *what you have made happen for others, God will make happen for you.*

As I said earlier, this principle works both ways, for good or bad. Remember the story of Jacob in the Bible? He deceived his dying father to receive the blessing that should have been his brother's. But only a few years later, Jacob was deceived by his uncle, Laban. After working seven years to gain the hand of the fair Rachel in marriage, Jacob was given the older sister, Leah. And he had to work seven more years for the girl he really wanted. What he made happen to someone else—deception— happened to him.

It also happens for good. Read 1 Kings 17:8-16 and you will find a fascinating success story. When a poor widow risked personal starvation in order to "create a success situation" for the prophet Elijah, God made that same miracle provision happen to her. *What she made happen for Elijah, God made happen for her!*

Though Job had experienced tremendous tragedies in his personal life, he got his mind off his own troubles, and began to pray for his friends instead. Then his own miracle happened to him—

The Lord turned *His* captivity! "And the Lord turned the captivity of Job, when he prayed for his friends: also the Lord gave Job twice as much as he had before" (Job 42:10).

Some time after God dealt with me so strongly on this subject, I was ministering in New Orleans, Louisiana. I urged the congregation to concentrate their efforts on making others successful, and God would make them successful. One young man really took my challenge to heart. He decided to put the principle to work with his boss.

He went to his employer and said, "I want to be your 'success-maker.' I want to make you more successful than you have ever been—the best boss you have ever been. I want you to make more money than you have ever made before. *Just tell me what I can do to help you be more successful. Give me some of your most difficult tasks* to do so you will be free to become more productive."

The young man's boss was completely shocked. He said, "No one has ever said that to me before. Tell me, *why* do you want to make me successful? *What do you want out of it?*"

The boy said, "I believe if I make you successful, then *God* will make me successful. If I help you to make more money for this business, then you will be able to pay me more. You'll be more successful, and so will I. I have wanted to make $6 an hour instead of $5. If I help you reach your goal you'll probably be able to help me achieve mine."

The boss said, "You will get your raise today. Anyone who cares about my success that much is surely worth $6 an hour!"

I believe with all my heart that this is one of the laws of God: *What You Make Happen For Others, God Will Make Happen For You.* Let this principle become part of the fabric of your understanding, and it will become a Golden Key in your hand to open every Room of Success you come to.

So start now. Concentrate on the success of those around you. How can you make your wife, your husband, your children more successful? How can you help your business or *employer* succeed in a greater way? What can you do to bless your church? Look for *new* ways to make everybody around you more successful. When you find such an opportunity, *be quick to carry it out.*

As you make them successful, God will bless you with success. "What You Make Happen For Others, God Will Make Happen For You" (Ephesians 6:8).

Where Do You Go From Here?

I've poured out my soul and a part of my very life to you in the pages of this book. I've shared in these pages what has taken many years to learn. And it is my heartfelt prayer that God will use this book to inspire you and challenge you to find the success He has for you.

Let's take a moment to review the basic truths God anointed me to include in the chapter:

First, God Wants You Successful. He wants your success to serve as an example of what He can do in a person's life. He wants you to succeed so you can provide for your family and be a strong spiritual leader for your loved ones. He wants your financial success to become a tool to help accomplish the Great Commission.

Second, We Defined What Success Is. *Success is achieving the goals God has for you as a person.* It is wanting what you get instead of getting what you want. It is not a destination, but the enjoyment experienced on the journey. And it is finding fulfillment in every part of life—spiritual, physical, mental, financial, social and family.

Third, God's Golden Key To Your Success Is Understanding. Solomon could have asked for—and received—anything he wanted, including riches, power, or fame, but he chose the Master Key of Understanding. As he used that key, he received all the other things as a bonus. What is Understanding? It is learning to interpret life as God does—to *see* through His eyes, to *hear* through His ears, to *comprehend* with His mind. *It is this ability that produces success in every area of your life.*

Fourth, Where Does Understanding Come From? It is a gift that only God can give. And He bestows it upon us through His Word. So studying and feeding upon the Word produces Understanding in us. And, Understanding produces success.

Fifth, *Developing A New Picture Of Yourself* Is The Way To Begin Moving Into The Realm Of Success. Stop looking at the ugly, distorted, defeated picture of yourself which satan would have you see. Instead, see yourself the way God sees you—full of potential and promise. See yourself in the image of God. What is God like? Exactly like His Son, Jesus, Who *was* and *is* the supreme Success-Maker.

Sixth, Learn That What You Make Happen For Others, God Will Make Happen For You. As you concentrate on putting good things into the lives of those around you, your own life will be filled with good things. As you create success for others, you find yourself living in a zone of success.

Having read these truths, where do you go from here? How can you apply them to your life to receive the most benefit?

Review and study each chapter of this book often. No doubt you will see some things you overlooked before—some of the truths will "dawn" on you in a new way.

By the end of the week, these principles of *Wisdom for Winning* will have become a habitual part of your thinking. You will already be noticing a difference in your outlook and your feelings. You will be on your way to success.

By the way, this book is not a complete study of success by any means. You will think of your own examples to further illustrate every point. You can find dozens of scriptures that expand and further develop every truth.

And this is exactly what you should do. Let God write a *new* book of success in your own life and heart. As it happens, *let me know about it.* Share with me what you learn about success just as I have shared with you. We will both be the richer for it.

Let me end this chapter with an admonition from the Word of God: "This book of the law shall not depart out of thy mouth; but thou shalt meditate therein day and night, that thou mayest observe to do according to all that is written therein: for then thou shalt make thy way prosperous, and then thou shalt have good success" (Joshua 1:8).

Remember...

God made you to soar...not sink!

God made you to climb...not crawl!

WISDOM PRINCIPLE 66

The Seasons Of Your Life Will Change Every Time You Decide To Use Your Faith.

God made you to fly...not fall!

God made you to stand... not stumble!

May God bless you as you become more POWER CONSCIOUS and live in the level of success HE has designed just for you.

∾ 25 ∾

WELCOME TO A WINNER'S WORLD

I am so excited for you! The fact that you are holding this book in your hand shows *you are headed in the right direction*...with the *right goals*...and you are willing to maintain your motivation by *keeping informed.* Remember: the difference between failure and success in life is information. 1) Information you *receive.* 2) Information you *believe.*

As you begin to act upon this information, you will become more confident, creative and energized.

WELCOME...I say, "Welcome!" because you have just entered into a new zone of happiness: victorious and successful living through Jesus Christ.

WINNER...I say, "Winner," because you are exactly that! An overcomer. A conqueror. A Victor!

WORLD...I say, "World," because you are a new citizen in a new domain...the kingdom of God.

YOUR SUCCESS IN LIFE depends on making the right choices. There are many things in which you have no choice. For instance, you cannot choose your parents, nor the color of your eyes, not even the color of your skin! However, for the *important* things that really determine your happiness, *you have the right to choose!*

And may I congratulate you! *You made the right*

choice. You chose the *right* way. The Way of hope. The Way of light. The Way of God...*The Way of the Winner.* Jesus said, "...I am the Way, the Truth, and the Life" (John 14:6).

You have received *Jesus* as your personal Savior. You have received *forgiveness* of every past sin. You have *crowned Him* King of your life.

You are *a new creation.*

In this simple step toward God, you have now discovered the *secret of success.* You are no longer a *slave* of sin, but a *son* of God!

Your decision to *experience* the Person of Jesus... and daily practice His principles in building a successful life reveals four beautiful qualities already inside you.

1.   You Have A Lot Of Awareness. You recognized the emptiness in your life. You were not blind to your own inner *longing.* You knew where to find the *answer.*

2.   You Have A Lot Of Honesty In You. You were willing to *say,* "God, I really need You." You refused to deceive yourself.

3.   You Are Showing A Lot Of Courage. You counted the *cost.* You were willing to pay the price (see Luke 14:28). Pride, past prejudices and inner fears did not stop you from total *surrender* to your Creator. That's *courage.*

4.   You Are Using A Lot Of Faith Already. Your faith pleases God: 1) You believe that He *exists.* 2) You believe that He *rewards.* "But without faith it is impossible to please Him; for he that cometh to God must believe that He is, and that He is a rewarder of them that diligently seek Him" (Hebrews 11:6).

These qualities confirm that you are on the right road. *You have what it takes to win!* Regardless of failures and wrong decisions in the past, you have now headed in the *right direction.* You are in a winner's world!

12 Things You Can Now Expect From God

1.   **His Ready Ear To Listen:** "...Thou wilt prepare their heart, Thou wilt cause thine ear to hear" (Psalm 10:17; also see Psalm 94:9).

2.   **His Watchful Eye:** "Behold, the eye of the Lord is upon them that fear Him, upon them that hope in His mercy" (Psalm 33:18; also see Psalm 94:9).

3.   **His Forgiveness:** "If we confess our sins, He is faithful and just to forgive us our sins, and to cleanse us from all unrighteousness" (1 John 1:9; also see Psalm 86:5).

4.   **His Guidance:** "And the Lord shall guide thee continually, and satisfy thy soul in drought" (Isaiah 58:11).

5.   **Inner Peace In Your Heart:** "Peace I leave with you, my peace I give unto you" (John 14:27; also see Philippians 4:7).

6.   **Inner Joy In Your Spirit:** "Therefore with joy shall ye draw water out of the wells of salvation" (Isaiah 12:3; also see John 15:11).

7.   **His Protection:** "There shall no evil befall thee, neither shall any plague come nigh thy dwelling" (Psalm 91:10; also see Psalm 32:7).

8.   **New Power To Overcome Sin:** "Ye are of God, little children, and have overcome them:

because greater is He that is in you, than he that is in the world" (1 John 4:4; also see Ephesians 3:20).

9. **Physical Healing In Your Body:** "...I am the Lord that healeth thee" (Exodus 15:26; also see Psalm 103:3; Matthew 8:16).

10. **Inner Healing In Your Broken Heart:** "He healeth the broken in heart, and bindeth up their wounds" (Psalm 147:3).

"The Lord is nigh unto them that are of a broken heart; and saveth such as be of a contrite spirit" (Psalm 34:18).

11. **His Consistency And Faithfulness:** "But the Lord is faithful, Who shall stablish you, and keep you from evil" (2 Thessalonians 3:3).

"I am with you alway, even unto the end of the world" (Matthew 28:20).

12. **His Wisdom For Living:** "But of Him are ye in Christ Jesus, Who of God is made unto us wisdom, and righteousness, and sanctification, and redemption" (1 Corinthians 1:30).

Power-Keys You Can Use

"Let us hear the conclusion of the whole matter: Fear God, and keep His commandments: for this is the whole duty of man" (Ecclesiastes 12:13).

"He hath shewed thee, O man, what is good; and what doth the Lord require of thee, but to do justly, and to love mercy, and to walk humbly with thy God?" (Micah 6:8).

Accepting Christ is instantaneous. However, it takes time and discipline on your part to become a mature and powerful believer. Here are some power keys you must remember.

6 Power Keys You Must Remember

1.   God-Consciousness. Continuously center your thoughts on God and Scriptural truth. This will crowd out wrong thinking, empower you during temptation and develop Wisdom for important decisions.

2.   Your Personal Prayer Life. Set up a *place* and a daily *time* for visiting with the Holy Spirit. Keep a list of names of those you pray for. Don't stay in an "asking posture"—learn to praise and thank Him for past answers!

3.   Your Daily Bible Reading Habit. Establish a *place, time* and *system.* Early morning is usually the best time because you have placed *mind-pictures* of truth into your spirit for the rest of the day. *Mark* your Bible. Take notes. Don't miss a single day.

4.   Godly Friendships. "He that walketh with wise men shall be wise: but a companion of fools shall be destroyed" (Proverbs 13:20). Be *selective.* Friends will *add to* or *take away* from your life.

5.   A Teachable Spirit. Several years ago a young lady approached me about a questionable activity in her life. She accepted my counsel. Today, she is a victorious and successful Christian: "A wise man will *hear*" (Proverbs 1:5). Through instruction and even criticism, we grow in grace and humility.

6.   A Winner's Mentality. Stop thinking about obstacles and start thinking about your *opportunities.* Talk *positive* words. Think good things about yourself and others. Stop complaining! Project enthusiasm! Avoid negative and depressing conversations. *Dominate your turf!* Be aggressively happy!

Recently, I was in a garden of beautiful flowers. While admiring their beauty, I noticed the gardener pulling up weeds that had grown up around them. As weeds choke out the life of a beautiful flower, there are things that we must remove in order to grow. To guarantee maturity and a winning life, you must eliminate the weeds.

6 Things You Must Eliminate From Your Life

1. **Wrong Relationships.** Ask yourself: "Will this friendship bring me *closer* to Jesus? Or will it *soil* the beauty of what God has begun?" Get rid of anything that clouds your mind or spirit.

2. **Moral Impurity.** Nothing can destroy your testimony and inner joy faster than immorality. When satan plants the "seed" of a bad thought in your mind, immediately *resist* it. Exercise your authority! Say: "satan, I bind you and resist your ungodly suggestions. I am a child of God walking in the power of the Holy Spirit. I cast your thought back to you. I am a new creation in Jesus!" Immediately, thank God *aloud* for good, wholesome thoughts.

3. **Ungodly Mind-Manipulators.** We are influenced greatly by what we *see and hear:* "Mine eye affecteth mine heart" (Lamentations 3:51). Depressing television shows, sensual music and suggestive books guarantee spiritual suicide. Replace these by saturating your life and home with wholesome books, tapes and Christian materials.

4. **Negative Conversation.** Words

WISDOM PRINCIPLE 67

Never Stay Where God Has Not Assigned You.

minister life or death (see Proverbs 18:21). *Put off* the former conversation. Ephesians 4:29 instructs: "Let no corrupt communication proceed out of your mouth, but that which is good to the use of edifying, that it may minister grace unto the hearers." Psalm 50:23 says: "...to him that ordereth his conversation aright will I show the salvation of God." Insist on positive and uplifting conversation.

5. **Bitterness And All Other Sin.** In Ephesians 4:31 Paul tells us: "Let all bitterness, and wrath, and anger, and clamour, and evil speaking, be put away from you." Bitterness is like a cancerous sore that deteriorates the inward soul of man. Sin is the deceptive snare that poisons the possibilities of a would-be winner. It promises *roses,* but delivers *thorns.* Repent and ask God to pour out His love through you to others.

6. **Time Wasters.** God is a Planner. From the creation of a world in seven days, including a rest zone, to a scheduled rapture, even a marriage supper of the Lamb projected thousands of years in advance, it is easy to conclude that our Father is a Master in details, goal-setting, priorities and order. Learn to avoid non-essentials, and energy wasters. *Make your time count:* "See then that ye walk circumspectly, not as fools, but as wise, Redeeming the time, because the days are evil" (Ephesians 5:15,16). Chart your course hourly. Daily. Monthly. Stay on target. Schedule every small success—

literally. Time spent with *God,* time spent with *others,* and time for *yourself.*

3 Things You Must Consecrate To God

1. **Your Talents And Abilities.** Every human is born with God-given gifts. It is up to you to *discover* and *develop* what God gave to you (read Matthew 25:14-29.) *You* are responsible for *you.*

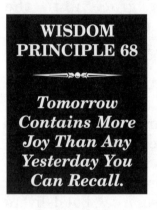

WISDOM PRINCIPLE 68

Tomorrow Contains More Joy Than Any Yesterday You Can Recall.

Whether you possess genius in music, speaking, mechanics, sports, management, or volunteer work in a ministry...*you are here on purpose.* Be the best at what you do. Don't just put God in first place, put Him every place "...whatsoever ye do, do all to the glory of God:" (1 Corinthians 10:31).

2. **Your Job And Career.** "...ye shall rejoice in all that ye put your hand unto" (Deuteronomy 12:7). God wants you happy with your job! If you are not excited about going to work each day, something is wrong. Does *a lack of knowledge* intimidate you? *Consult your boss* for greater understanding. *Invest time* in learning more about your field. We were made to *reach.* Like a dear friend of mine says, "Like rubber bands, we are at our best when we are *stretched* to some degree." *Information* breeds *motivation.* On the other hand, thousands are trapped in undesirable careers through *fear.* Fear of failure, fear of the unknown. Dare to *step up and out* into new opportunities! Dare to try! *The dreamer, the* *achiever, the adventurer is destined for supernatural success.*

3. **Your Finances.** Your attitude toward money reveals your true values. Jesus talked about it. The apostle Paul talked about it. Money is *important.* It is your time, your toil, your sweat, your energy...it is *you.* It is the *power part* of you. With it you bargain and exchange your way through life. It is *your food.* Your *shelter.* Your *clothing. What you do with it makes all the difference in the world to God.* Abraham gave tithe in thanksgiving for his blessing. In Matthew 23:23 Jesus commended the Pharisees for doing the same. Tithing is *not* the payment of a debt to God. All of it belongs to Him.

Tithing is the *acknowledgment* of the debt. Offerings to God are Seeds planted in holy soil; and He personally guarantees a bountiful return (read Deuteronomy 8:18; Deuteronomy 28:1-14; Luke 6:38, 2 Corinthians 9:6; Malachi 3:10,11).

2 Success-Forces You Must Activate

1. **Your Words:** "The mouth of the just bringeth forth wisdom" (Proverbs 10:31). "...he that winneth souls is wise" (Proverbs 11:30). Proverbs 10:20 says: "The tongue of the just is as choice silver."

Words have power. Men talk about the things they *love* whether it be football, children or pizza! True born-again believers thrive on God-talk! You should want to talk about the promises and power of God to Christians and non-Christians alike.

The secrets of man will surface through the mouth. Matthew 12:34 says: "...out of the abundance of the heart the mouth speaketh." Dare to speak out to others about what God has done in your life: "Let the redeemed of the Lord SAY so" (Psalm 107:2). Tell your family. Your friends. Your fellow workers. With gentle, loving and kind words, portray with authority the life of Jesus within you.

    2.   **Your Relationships:** "He that walketh with wise men shall be wise" (Proverbs 13:20).

    Identify and associate with quality people. This is one of the great secrets of success. Surround yourself with a "Success-Climate" of Jesus-lovers. You need to have a church "home." For growth, stability and ministry God established the local church and pastor for your own spiritual success. Do not select a church based only upon friendships, convenience or traditions. *Seek God.* Listen to the Holy Spirit. *He knows where He can use you best.* Be loyal and committed to that congregation. In attendance, involvement and financial support, *stand behind that pastor* with your faithfulness.

A Final Word

    Read this book at least once a week for the next few months. As it gets into your mind and spirit, your spiritual growth will amaze you! A dynamic vitality will develop that will astound even your friends. *You truly will be a winner.*

    My own goal in life is to please the Holy Spirit completely...stay in The Secret Place...and write the Wisdom Keys that enable others to succeed. Please feel free to write me and share your prayer needs. I believe and practice the power of daily prayer. I will pray for you. I will write you back and stand in agreement for the Most Uncommon Year of Success You Have Ever Known.

WISDOM PRINCIPLES WORTH REMEMBERING

1. A Productive Life Is Not An Accident.
2. Never Speak Words That Make Satan Think He's Winning.
3. Adversity Is The Breeding Ground For Miracles.
4. Those Who Are Unwilling To Lose, Rarely Do.
5. Happiness Is Movement Toward That Which Is Right.
6. Happiness Occurs When You Move Toward Anything That Is Right For You.
7. No One Has Been A Loser Longer Than Satan.
8. Those Who Do Not Respect Your Time Will Not Respect Your Wisdom Either.
9. Stop Looking At What You See And Start Looking At What You Can Have.
10. Intolerance Of The Present Creates A Future.
11. Forgiveness Is Not A Suggestion, But A Requirement.
12. Whoever Cannot Increase You, Will Eventually Decrease You.
13. Today Is The Tomorrow You Talked About Yesterday.
14. Your Words Are Signposts To Others — Pointing In The Direction Your Life Is Moving.
15. You Will Never Reach Your Potential Until Your Priorities Become Habitual.
16. Your Life Assignment Is Usually Whatever Creates The Highest Level Of Joy Within You.
17. You Will Never Possess What You Are Unwilling To Pursue.
18. Your Pain Can Become Your Passage To The Greatest Miracle Of Your Life.
19. You Will Never Reach The Palace Talking Like A Peasant.

20. Stop Looking At Where You Have Been And Start Looking At Where You Can Be.
21. Your Words Are Deciding Your Future.
22. A True Winner Will Never Advertise Nor Magnify His Personal Weaknesses.
23. You Can Only Move Away From A Bad Thought By Deliberately Moving Toward A Good One.
24. You Cannot Reap Grapes Until You Have Sowed Grapes Into Others.
25. Your Contribution To Others Determines God's Contribution To You.
26. Any Disorder In Your Life Can Create The Death Of Your Dream.
27. The Proof Of Desire Is Pursuit.
28. What You Think About Money Often Reveals What You Really Think About Life.
29. Whatever You Think About Most Is Really Your God.
30. Prosperity Is Simply Having Enough Of God's Provisions To Complete His Instructions For Your Life.
31. Selfishness Is Depriving Another To Benefit Yourself.
32. Giving Is Proof That You Have Conquered Greed.
33. When You Let Go Of What Is In Your Hand, God Will Let Go Of What Is In His Hand For You.
34. When What You Hold In Your Hand Is Not Enough To Be A Harvest, Make It A Seed.
35. Your Seed Is Like A Purchase Order In The Warehouse Of Heaven...Authorizing Miracle Packages To Be Sent Into Your Life.
36. Satan's Favorite Entry Into Your Life Is Usually

Through Those Closest To You.

37. Confidentiality Is One Of The Most Treasured Gifts You Can Give To Another.

38. Stop Looking At Where You Have Been And Begin Looking At Where You Are Going.

39. What Your Mind Cannot Master, It Will Eventually Resent.

40. Anger Will Never Create Permanent Cooperation From Another.

41. The Broken Become Masters At Mending.

42. Don't Poison Your Future With The Pain Of The Past.

43. What You Fail To Destroy, Will Eventually Destroy You.

44. Depression Will Always Follow Any Decision To Avoid A Priority.

45. When *Fatigue* Walks In, *Faith* Walks Out.

46. Loneliness Is Not A Loss Of Affection But The Loss Of Direction.

47. Immaturity Is The Inability To Delay Self-Gratification.

48. Your Self-Worth Is Not Determined By Your Past Mistakes, But By Your Willingness To Recognize Them.

49. Repentance Is Always The First Step To Recovery.

50. Failure Will Last Only As Long As You Permit It.

51. Men Do Not Really Decide Their Future...They Decide Their Habits—Then, Their Habits Decide Their Future.

52. Yesterday's Failure...*Can* Become The Catalyst For Tomorrow's Success.

53. If God Cushioned Every Blow, You Would Never Learn To Grow.

54. Confession Is A Faith-Releaser Into Total Restoration.
55. Your Contribution To Others Determines What God Will Contribute To You.
56. Your Life Will Always Move In The Direction Of Your Strongest Thought.
57. You Are Never As Far From A Miracle As It First Appears.
58. You'll Never Leave Where You Are, Until You Decide Where You'd Rather Be.
59. The Picture That Stays In Your Mind Will Happen In Time.
60. When You Get Into The Word—The Word Will Get Into You.
61. Pain Is Often A Bridge, Not A Barricade To Success.
62. You Create A Season Of Success Every Time You Complete An Instruction From God.
63. You Will Always Struggle, Subconsciously To Become The Self-Portrait You Believe Yourself To Be.
64. The Day You Make A Decision About Your Life Is The Day Your World Will Change.
65. Your Harvest Will Always Come Through The Door Of Someone In Trouble, Who Is Needing Your Help.
66. The Season Of Your Life Will Change Every Time You Decide To Use Your Faith.
67. Never Stay Where God Has Not Assigned You.
68. Tomorrow Contains More Joy Than Any Yesterday You Can Recall.

DECISION

DR. MIKE MURDOCK

is in tremendous demand as one of the most dynamic speakers in America today.

Will You Accept Jesus As Your Personal Savior Today?

The Bible says, "That if thou shalt confess with thy mouth the Lord Jesus, and shalt believe in thine heart that God hath raised Him from the dead, thou shalt be saved" (Romans 10:9).

Pray this prayer from your heart today!

"Dear Jesus, I believe that You died for me and rose again on the third day. I confess I am a sinner...I need Your love and forgiveness... Come into my heart. Forgive my sins. I receive Your eternal life. Confirm Your love by giving me peace, joy and supernatural love for others. Amen."

More than 14,000 audiences in 38 countries have attended his meetings and seminars. Hundreds of invitations come to him from churches, colleges and business corporations. He is a noted author of over 140 books, including the best sellers, *"The Leadership Secrets of Jesus"* and *"Secrets of the Richest Man Who Ever Lived."* Thousands view his weekly television program, *"Wisdom Keys with Mike Murdock."* Many attend his Schools of Wisdom that he hosts in major cities of America.

☐ Yes, Mike! I made a decision to accept Christ as my personal Savior today. Please send me my free gift of your book, *"31 Keys to a New Beginning"* to help me with my new life in Christ. *(B-48)*

NAME _____ BIRTHDAY _____

ADDRESS _____

CITY _____ STATE _____ ZIP _____

PHONE _____ E-MAIL _____

Mail form to:
The Wisdom Center • *4051 Denton Hwy.* • *Ft. Worth, TX 76117*
Phone: 1-888-WISDOM-1 (1-888-947-3661)
Website: thewisdomcenter.tv

227

DR. MIKE MURDOCK

1 Has embraced his Assignment to Pursue...Proclaim...and Publish the Wisdom of God to help people achieve their dreams and goals.

2 Began full-time evangelism at the age of 19, which has continued since 1966.

3 Has traveled and spoken to more than 14,000 audiences in 38 countries, including East and West Africa, the Orient and Europe.

4 Noted author of over 140 books, including best sellers, "Wisdom For Winning," "Dream Seeds" and "The Double Diamond Principle."

5 Created the popular "Topical Bible" series for Businessmen, Mothers, Fathers, Teenagers; "The One-Minute Pocket Bible" series, and "The Uncommon Life" series.

6 Has composed more than 5,700 songs such as "I Am Blessed," "You Can Make It," "God Rides On Wings Of Love" and "Jesus Just The Mention Of Your Name," recorded by many gospel artists.

7 Is the Founder of The Wisdom Center, in Fort Worth, Texas.

8 Has a weekly television program called "Wisdom Keys With Mike Murdock."

9 Has appeared often on TBN, CBN, BET and other television network programs.

10 Is a Founding Trustee on the Board of International Charismatic Bible Ministries with Oral Roberts.

11 Has had more than 3,500 accept the call into full-time ministry under his ministry.

THE MINISTRY

1 **Wisdom Books & Literature** - Over 140 best-selling Wisdom Books and 70 Teaching Tape Series.

2 **Church Crusades** - Multitudes are ministered to in crusades and seminars throughout America in "The Uncommon Wisdom Conferences." Known as a man who loves pastors, he has focused on church crusades for 38 years.

3 **Music Ministry** - Millions have been blessed by the anointed songwriting and singing of Mike Murdock, who has made over 15 music albums and CDs available.

4 **Television** - "Wisdom Keys With Mike Murdock," a nationally-syndicated weekly television program.

5 **The Wisdom Center** - The Ministry Offices of The Mike Murdock Evangelistic Association where Schools Of Wisdom have been held.

6 **Schools of the Holy Spirit** - Mike Murdock hosts Schools of the Holy Spirit in many churches to mentor believers on the Person and companionship of the Holy Spirit.

7 **Schools of Wisdom** - In many major cities Mike Murdock hosts Schools of Wisdom for those who want personalized and advanced training for achieving "The Uncommon Dream."

8 **Missions Outreach** - Dr. Murdock's overseas outreaches to 38 countries have included crusades in East and West Africa, South America, the Orient and Europe.

What Matters Most.

- ▶ 17 Facts You Should Know About The Holy Spirit

- ▶ The Greatest Weapon The Holy Spirit Has Given You

- ▶ 15 Facts About The Love Of The Holy Spirit

- ▶ 17 Facts Every Christian Should Know About Grieving The Holy Spirit

- ▶ 17 Facts You Should Know About The Anointing

- ▶ 3 Ways The Holy Spirit Will Talk To You

- ▶ 8 Important Facts About Your Assignment

The Holy Spirit, The Assignment, and The Seed. These three vital areas are the most important things in your life. Mike Murdock addresses each topic in a profound and dynamic way. In this volume he carefully lays out the Wisdom Secrets to successful Living. Your understanding will be energized as knowledge enters your heart and you begin to find your Assignment in the purpose of God.

The Wisdom Center

$10

B-101

Wisdom Is The Principal Thing

Add 10% For S/H

Learn From The Greatest.

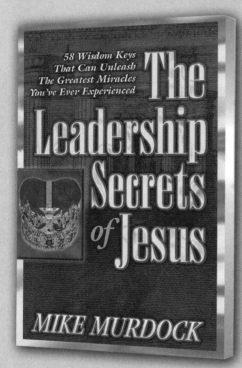

58 Wisdom Keys That Can Unleash The Greatest Miracles You've Ever Experienced

The Leadership Secrets of Jesus

MIKE MURDOCK

▶ The Secret Of Handling Rejection

▶ How To Deal With The Mistakes Of Others

▶ 5 Power Keys For Effective Delegation To Others

▶ The Key To Developing Great Faith

▶ The Greatest Qualities Of Champions

▶ The Secret Of The Wealthy

▶ Four Goal-Setting Techniques

▶ Ten Facts Jesus Taught About Money

In this dynamic and practical guidebook Mike Murdock points you directly to Jesus, the Ultimate Mentor. You'll take just a moment every day to reflect on His life and actions. And when you do, you'll discover all the key skills and traits that Jesus used... the powerful "leadership secrets" that build true, lasting achievement. Explore them. Study them. Put them to work in your own life and your success will be assured!

Somebody's Future
Will Not Begin Until You Enter.

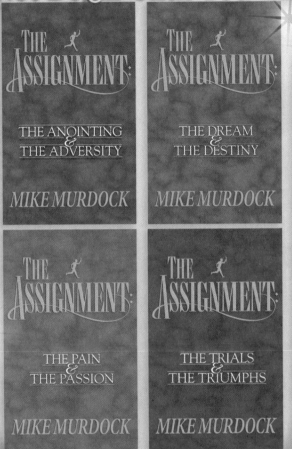

THIS COLLECTION INCLUDES 4 DIFFERENT BOOKS CONTAINING UNCOMMON WISDOM FOR DISCOVERING YOUR LIFE ASSIGNMENT

▶ How To Achieve A God-Given Dream And Goal

▶ How To Know Who Is Assigned To You

▶ The Purpose And Rewards Of An Enemy

The Wisdom Center
Book Pak
WBL-14 **/$30**
Buy 3-Get 1 Free
($10 Each/$40 Value!)
Wisdom Is The Principal Thing

Add 10% For S/H

Getting Past The Pain.

- ▶ 6 Essential Facts That Must Be Faced When Recovering From Divorce
- ▶ 4 Forces That Guarantee Career Success
- ▶ 3 Ways Crisis Can Help You
- ▶ 4 Reasons You Are Experiencing Opposition To Your Assignment
- ▶ How To Predict The 6 Seasons Of Attack On Your Life
- ▶ 4 Keys That Can Shorten Your Present Season Of Struggle
- ▶ 2 Important Facts You Must Know About Battle & Warfare
- ▶ 6 Weapons Satan Uses To Attack Marriages

Wisdom For Crisis Times
Master Keys For Success In Times of Change
Mike Murdock

Wisdom For Crisis Times will give you the answers to the struggle you are facing now, and any struggle you could ever face. Dr. Murdock presents practical steps to help you walk through your "Seasons of Fire."

The Wisdom Center
Book B-40 / $9
Six Audio Tapes TS-40 / $30
Wisdom Is The Principal Thing

- ▶ 96 Wisdom Keys from God's Word will direct you into the success that God intended for your life. This teaching will unlock the door to your personal happiness, peace of mind, fulfillment and success.

Add 10% For S/H

 THE WISDOM CENTER
4051 Denton Highway • Fort Worth, TX 76117

1-888-WISDOM1
(1-888-947-3661)

Website:
WWW.THEWISDOMCENTER

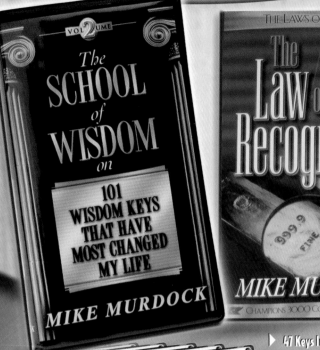
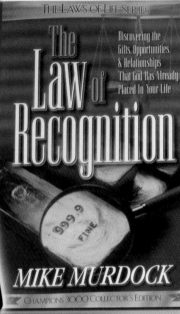

Financial Success.

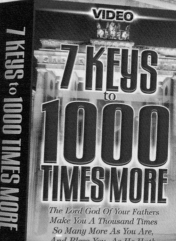

31 REAON PEOPLE DO NOT RECEIVE THEIR FINANCIAL HARVE$T

MIKE MURDOCK

7 KEYS to 1000 TIMES MORE

The Lord God Of Your Fathers Make You A Thousand Times So Many More As You Are, And Bless You, As He Hath Promised You!
Deuteronomy 1:11

MIKE MURDOCK

▶ 8 Scriptural Reasons You Should Pursue Financial Prosperity

▶ The Secret Prayer Key You Need When Making A Financial Request To God

▶ The Weapon Of Expectation And The 5 Miracles It Unlocks

▶ How To Discern Those Who Qualify To Receive Your Financial Assistance

▶ How To Predict The Miracle Moment God Will Schedule Your Financial Breakthrough

▶ Habits Of Uncommon Achievers

▶ The Greatest Success Law I Ever Discovered

▶ How To Discern Your Place Of Assignment, The Only Place Financial Provision Is Guaranteed

▶ 3 Secret Keys In Solving Problems For Others

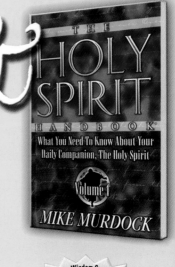

The Uncommon Woman

- ▸ **Master Keys In Understanding The Man In Your Life**
- ▸ **The One Thing Every Man Attempts To Move Away From**
- ▸ **The Dominant Difference Between A Wrong Woman And A Right Woman**
- ▸ **What Causes Men To Withdraw**

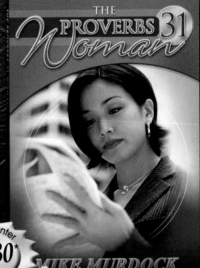

MIKE MURDOCK

THE WISDOM FOR WOMEN SERIES

THIRTY - ONE SECRETS of an UNFORGETTABLE WOMAN

Master Secrets from the Life of Ruth

THE WISDOM CENTER
MIKE MURDOCK • P.O. Box 99 • Denton, Texas

31 Secrets of an Unforgettable Woman

The Wisdom Center
6 Tapes | **$30***
PAK-009
Wisdom Is The Principal Thing

Free Book Enclosed!
Wisdom Is The Principal Thing

Add 10% For S/H

*This offer expires December 31, 2004

 **THE WISDOM CENTER**
4051 Denton Highway • Fort Worth, TX 76117

1-888-WISDOM1
(1-888-947-3661)

Website:
THEWISDOMCENTER.TV

E

GIFTS OF WISDOM...

THE BU$INE$$ BIBLE YO
HAVE ALWAYS WANTED.

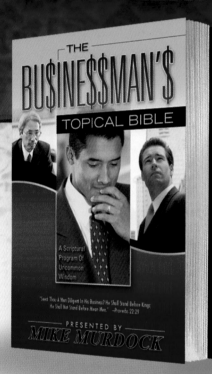

THE
BU$INE$$MAN'$
TOPICAL BIBLE

A Scriptural Program Of Uncommon Wisdom

"Seest Thou A Man Diligent In His Business? He Shall Stand Before Kings; He Shall Not Stand Before Mean Men." –Proverbs 22:29

PRESENTED BY
MIKE MURDOCK

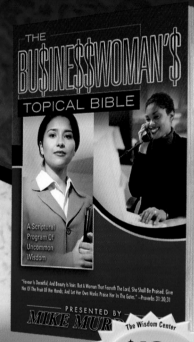

THE
BU$INE$$WOMAN'$
TOPICAL BIBLE

A Scriptural Program Of Uncommon Wisdom

"Favour Is Deceitful, And Beauty Is Vain: But A Woman That Feareth The Lord, She Shall Be Praised. Give Her Of The Fruit Of Her Hands; And Let Her Own Works Praise Her In The Gates." –Proverbs 31:30,31

PRESENTED BY
MIKE MUR

GIFTS OF WISDOM....

Pocket Power!

- 1 Minute Pocket Bible For Achievers (B-50 / $5.00)
- 1 Minute Pocket Bible For Fathers (B-51 / $5.00)
- 1 Minute Pocket Bible For Mothers (B-52 / $5.00)
- 1 Minute Pocket Bible For Teenagers (B-53 / $5.00)
- 1 Minute Pocket Bible For Men (B-60 / $5.00)
- 1 Minute Pocket Bible For Business Professionals (B-62 / $5.00)
- 1 Minute Pocket Bible For Women (B-61 / $5.00)
- 1 Minute Pocket Bible For Truckers (B-63 / $5.00)

The Wisdom Center

**WISDOM...
The Greatest
Gift Of All!**

Wisdom Is The Principal Thing

Add 10% For S/H

Quantity Prices Available Upon Request

THE WISDOM CENTER
4051 Denton Highway • Fort Worth, TX 76117

1-888-WISDOM1
(1-888-947-3661)

Website:
THEWISDOMCENTER.TV

G

What Every Parent Has Been Waiting For...

A 12-Month Family Mentorship Program.
Over 365 Chapters Of Wisdom For Every Day Of The Year.

GIFTS OF WISDOM...

SPECIALTY *Bibles*

*Each Book Sold Separately

► **The Businessman's Topical Bible** (B-33 / $10)
► **The Children's Topical Bible** (B-154 / $10)
► **The Father's Topical Bible** (B-35 / $10)
► **The Grandparent's Topical Bible** (B-34 / $10)
► **The Minister's Topical Bible** (B-32 / $10)
► **The Mother's Topical Bible** (B-36 / $10)
► **The New Believer's Topical Bible** (B-37 / $10)
► **The Seeds Of Wisdom Topical Bible** (B-31 / $10)
► **The Serviceman's Topical Bible** (B-138 / $10)

► **The Teen's Topical Bible** (B-30 / $10)
► **The Traveler's Topical Bible** (B-139 / $10)
► **The Widow's Topical Bible** (B-38 / $10)

The Wisdom Center
Only **$10** Each
Wisdom Is The Principal Thing

Add 10% For S/H

THE WISDOM CENTER
4051 Denton Highway • Fort Worth, TX 76117

1-888-WISDOM1
(1-888-947-3661)

Website:
THEWISDOMCENTER.TV

My Gift Of Appreciation...
The Wisdom Commentary

The Wisdom Commentary includes 52 topics...for mentoring your family every week of the year.

These topics include:

- Abilities
- Achievement
- Anointing
- Assignment
- Bitterness
- Blessing
- Career
- Change
- Children
- Dating
- Depression
- Discipline
- Divorce
- Dreams And Goals
- Enemy
- Enthusiasm
- Favor
- Finances
- Fools

- Giving
- Goal-Setting
- God
- Happiness
- Holy Spirit
- Ideas
- Intercession
- Jobs
- Loneliness
- Love
- Mentorship
- Ministers
- Miracles
- Mistakes
- Money
- Negotiation
- Prayer
- Problem-Solving
- Protégés

- Satan
- Secret Place
- Seed-Faith
- Self-Confidence
- Struggle
- Success
- Time-Management
- Understanding
- Victory
- Weaknesses
- Wisdom
- Word Of God
- Words
- Work

THE WISDOM COMMENTARY 1

B-136

Gift Of Appreciation
For Your Sponsorship Seed of $100 or More
Gift Of Appreciation

My Gift Of Appreciation To My Sponsors!
..Those Who Sponsor One Square Foot In
The Completion Of The Wisdom Center!

hank you so much for becoming a part of this wonderful project...The completion of The Wisdom Center! he total purchase and renovation cost of this facility (10,000 square feet) is just over $1,000,000. This is pproximately $100 per square foot. **The Wisdom Commentary is my Gift of Appreciation for your ponsorship Seed of $100...that sponsors one square foot of The Wisdom Center. Become a Sponsor!** You ill love this Volume 1, of The Wisdom Commentary. It is my exclusive Gift of Appreciation for The Wisdom ey Family who partners with me in the Work of God as a Sponsor.

Add 10% For S/H

 THE WISDOM CENTER
4051 Denton Highway • Fort Worth, TX 76117

**1-888-WISDOM1
(1-888-947-3661)**

Website:
THEWISDOMCENTER.TV

K

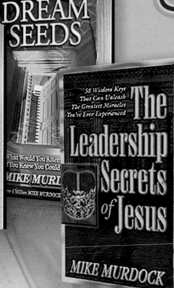
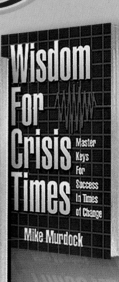

UNCOMMON WISDOM FOR UNCOMMON ACHIEVERS

Dream 7 PAK

- ► The Leadership Secrets Of Jesus (B-91 / $10)
- ► Dream Seeds (B-11 / $9)
- ► Secrets Of The Richest Man Who Ever Lived (B-99 / $10)
- ► The Assignment: The Dream And The Destiny, Volume 1 (B-74 / $10)
- ► The Holy Spirit Handbook (B-100 / $10)
- ► The Law Of Recognition (B-114 / $10)
- ► 31 Reasons People Do Not Receive Their Financial Harvest (B-82 / $12)

P  **THE WISDOM CENTER**
4051 Denton Highway • Fort Worth, TX 76117

1-888-WISDOM1
(1-888-947-3661)

Website:
THEWISDOMCENTER.TV